LOVE, LAUGH, BE

How I
Wound Up
With Nine
Amazing Kids
(When I Only
Knew About
Three)
And Other
Extraordinary
True Stories
That Matter

DR. BRIAR FLICKER-GROSSMAN

Paperback: ISBN: 978-1-7345130-0-4
Hardback: ISBN: 978-1-7345130-1-1
E-book: ISBN: 978-1-7345130-2-8

Library of Congress Control Number: 2020902490

Edited by Qat Wanders and Wandering Words Media
https://www.qatwanders.com

Photographer: Kit Karzen
https://www.kitkarzen.com

Cover Design by 100Covers.com
Interior Formatting by FormattedBooks.com

DEDICATION

This book is dedicated to my parents, my husband, and also my children… all of them, old and new, who teach me everyday about the power of love and inspire me always.

It is dedicated to all parents and all those who dream of being parents. It is dedicated to all the children, born and yet to be born, who bare the torch of humanity for all that will be.

"Love is old,
Love is new,
Love is all,
Love is you."
—"BECAUSE" BY JOHN LENNON
RELEASED SEPTEMBER 26, 1969
THE BEATLES- "ABBEY ROAD"

FREE!

A complimentary gift from me to you....
I just want to say thank you for buying my book.

Please Go To:
www.drbriar.com/freeaudible
to register for a FREE copy of the Audible version of
LOVE, LAUGH, BE...

—*Soon to be Released*—

Please note, a portion of the proceeds from sales
of this book will go to Homeless Not Toothless,
another remarkable child of mine.

CONTENTS

DEDICATION. III
INTRODUCTION. XV

PART I: MY BEGINNINGS

CHAPTER 1
Mom, Dad, and Me or Meet the Flickers Part I. 3

CHAPTER 2
Moving Right Along. 6

CHAPTER 3
In Tornado Land. 8

PART II: GOOD UNTIL I WASN'T—LOST REBEL

CHAPTER 4
Still Good 14

CHAPTER 5
Middle School Looms —Like Middle Earth 16

CHAPTER 6
Inklings of Trouble...
Little Teen, Little Troubles; Big Teen, Big Troubles 18

CHAPTER 7
Curiosity, Kisses, and Catastrophe 20

CHAPTER 8
Getting Banged Up Catches Up. 27

PART III: THE TURNAROUND

CHAPTER 9
Getting Help and Failing Forward 34

CHAPTER 10
Perchance to Dream—And Then to Understand. 37

CHAPTER 11
Venturing Out and Finding My Way 39

PART IV: MAGIC MOMENTS

CHAPTER 12
Finding Me. 48

CHAPTER 13
Rocking My World 49

CHAPTER 14
B'sheret—Destiny 54

CHAPTER 15
Love With Freedom and Ease. 58

CHAPTER 16

The Sperm Donor Dinner. 61

CHAPTER 17

Spring Break 63

CHAPTER 18

Meet The Flickers, Part II. 66

CHAPTER 19

Love and Marriage. 70

PART V: AND THEN WE WERE FIVE

CHAPTER 20

Getting Started 78

CHAPTER 21

And It Started With Sydney Rebecca Flicker Grossman 81

CHAPTER 22

My Family Grows, and So Do I: Eric Benjamin Flicker
Grossman, Pregnancy, and The Bradley Method. 87

CHAPTER 23

Giving Birth To A Philanthropy 97

CHAPTER 24

The Final Addition...
We Thought: Ari Max Flicker Grossman 101

PART VI: DARK TIMES...BIG BUMPS... LOVE DON'T FAIL ME NOW

CHAPTER 25
Let The Trials Begin—Loss 108

CHAPTER 26
The Ups And Downs
Of Business 112

CHAPTER 27
The S#%t Kept Hitting The Fan 119

CHAPTER 28
Surviving And Thriving 130

CHAPTER 29
More Ups and Downs 137

CHAPTER 30
One More Thing...Mamma 142

CHAPTER 31
Ari Falls Down, But He Gets Up Again and Again—
Learning From My Children 145

PART VII: SILVER LININGS: MAGIC MOMENTS WILL ALWAYS COME, GIVEN TIME

CHAPTER 32
Wedding Bells 162

CHAPTER 33
Babies Anyone? 165

CHAPTER 34

The Past Is Present 167

PART VIII: MEET THE KIDS

CHAPTER 35

The First Bunch 172

CHAPTER 36

The Second Bunch 184

PART IX: FROM GENERATION TO GENERATION

CHAPTER 37

Connecting 192

CHAPTER 38

A New Generation 195

PART X: THE END

CHAPTER 39

The End—But Only Of The Book 204

ACKNOWLEDGMENTS 209

ABOUT THE AUTHOR 213

INTRODUCTION

*"Somebody should tell us, right at the start of
our lives, that we are dying. Then we might
live life to the limit, every minute of every day.
Do it, I say. Whatever you want to do, do it
now. There are only so many tomorrows."*

—POPE PAUL VI

This book includes stories I have told over and over about childbirth, life coaching, and my own history. Its emotional subject matter is colored by the psychoanalytic world I grew up in. Its influence is woven throughout these pages.

Psychoanalysis presents a theory and practice for knowing and loving oneself and others, an approach I have found to be very meaningful and highly applicable. The key idea is that the unconscious plays an influential role in the choices we make and the actions we take. You will see throughout this book how some choices I made were driven unconsciously by self-destructive parts of me. As I came to know myself better over time, I made better, happier choices.

Another important component of psychoanalysis is the idea that our personalities are multifaceted. Through my experience, I have come to believe that we are always influenced by our internal voices, of which we have many. Within our minds, we have baby parts, our inner child, and versions of our parents that can be idealized or very critical and cruel, among others. We are also born with a part of our being that is intrinsically unique. I will speak, in probably unfamiliar ways, about the different voices in my mind—voices we all have. These aren't representations of multiple personalities or mental illness; they are our internal influencers, and they have served me well. I think you will see how these underlying ideas have helped me love, laugh, and be.

At times in my life, I have been ill with cancer, I have had emotional and real losses, and I have gone through financial bankruptcy—but at the end of the day, I never felt beaten. I have fallen and stayed in love for a lifetime. I have given birth to three wonderful children and wound up discovering I am the mother of many more. I love my family, my career, and every breath I am lucky enough to breathe, and a *big* part of my journey has been learning to love myself, including all my internal voices.

People have asked me to share my journey for many years—I think because it is about ordinary human extraordinariness. It is about frailty and strength, about struggle and the power of love. It is about "being," and making each moment count.

Love, laugh, be.

From me to you with love,
Briar

I
MY BEGINNINGS

"You only live once,
but if you do it right, once is enough."
—MAE WEST (1893-1980)
AMERICAN ACTRESS, SINGER, PLAYWRIGHT,
SCREENWRITER, COMEDIAN, AND SEX SYMBOL

1
MOM, DAD, AND ME OR MEET THE FLICKERS PART I

I slept in a drawer.

1960, Chicago, Illinois. Dad was in medical school, and my parents had been married just over a year. Dad was twenty-four, and Mom was twenty. They set a high bar. They didn't have much when I was born besides their romance and a desire to live the "American Dream."

Mom was artsy and edgy, even back then, and met my dad when he recognized his alma mater on her sweatshirt at a beach in Miami during spring break. He asked her out on the spot.

They had only a week together in Miami, but theirs was a fast and furious love affair. Afterward, they wrote to each other daily and tried to keep the relationship kindled, my dad from medical school in Chicago, my mom from Bard in upstate New York. Within a month or two, the way my dad tells it, he realized he didn't want to spend another day without my mom by his side.

He proposed to her, and three months after they met, they were married. In fact, they were married twice. They had a civil ceremony at my mother's home in the Catskills and a religious ceremony in deference to Dad's family. They returned, deeply in love, to Chicago to start their lives in Dad's teeny-tiny apartment.

Mom and Dad had only a few short blissful months alone together.

I was born thirteen months after their wedding(s). I feel a triumphant glee that I have known them almost as long as they have known each other. Such is the thrill of inclusion. The stories I have heard from my mom about her pregnancy and my birth have had a huge impact on how deeply connected I am to her, Dad, and my own life.

Mom told me she loved being pregnant with me and how easy it was. As a little girl, I felt a certain pride about that. I recall asking her at different times throughout my life about how I was born. Children, encouraged and unsuppressed, will naturally be curious about everything. This was first noted by the earliest psychoanalysts and psychologists. Sigmund Freud named it the epistemophilic instinct—in other words, natural curiosity.

My mother was a great storyteller when I was a little girl, and the story of my birth was one of my favorites. I loved when she told me her belly squeezed her when it was time for me to come out, and how exciting it was when Daddy drove her to the hospital where she would soon meet me. In 1960, fathers were nowhere to be found in labor or delivery rooms, unlike most hospitals today, where labor and delivery happen in one room, and fathers are welcome. Another standard operating procedure back then was to knock moms out for the birth of their babies, putting them into a deep 'twilight sleep.' Many moms woke up wondering if the baby they were handed was for sure really theirs—and as we now know, mistakes were indeed made, on occasion.

My mother wanted to be alert, informed, and ready. She studied Grantly Dick-Read's deep relaxation techniques during her pregnancy and read extensively about birth. Her only real worry was that my father would forget her glasses when they went to the hospital. She wanted to see my birth clearly. She would have been really mad if she missed it. Finally, the time came, and she didn't push long. In fact, when she started pushing, she felt eager and excited. Since my dad was an intern at the hospital, he was "allowed" in the delivery room and was right by her side, rooting her on. At the right moment, glasses on and a mirror rolled over, Mom and Dad gasped in awe as I emerged.

"Oh Briar," Dad would tell me when I was little. "How Mom and I wept at your birth. It was a miracle like nothing I had ever seen before."

"You cried? Did I hurt Mommy?"

"No," they explained. "We were just so happy you had joined the family."

That was the first time I recall understanding that crying can be for happiness and pleasure. I knew from that moment that I definitely wanted to be a mommy, grow a baby in my belly, and push, push, push that baby out of my vagina just like my mom did.

2
MOVING RIGHT ALONG

The first few years of my childhood had its ups and downs. I felt very loved and special to my parents. When I was one, we moved to Japan for four years where my father was a captain in the Air Force. He was to be a doctor on the base, and my mother would teach English to the Japanese locals. Along the way, my mother became pregnant with another baby. I recall, in misty mental snapshots, loving her growing belly.

My mom went into labor with her second baby, but my parents did not return from the hospital with a sibling for me. Horrified and so sad, I looked on when my parents came home empty-handed. When my mother gave birth to this baby, Israel, he had a lung abnormality called Hyaline Membrane Disease. This deadly problem would be curable only two years later, after Jackie Kennedy lost a baby to the same condition. Israel couldn't breathe and died when he was three days old.

At just under two years old, I didn't fully understand the situation, but I knew Mommy was very, very sad. I felt sad and scared to see my mommy so devastated, and was also hurt by my dad's pain and anguish. They were experiencing feelings I only came to identify much later as helplessness, grief, anger, and unfounded guilt.

I can tell you that I *was*, and preverbal small children *are*, taking in, thinking about, and feeling everything they encounter externally and internally. Unconsciously, it all moves forward through life-shaping moments that inform our future thoughts and feelings, sometimes for the better and sometimes not. But again, anything we want to understand and work on is available somewhere inside, ready and waiting.

I know now that my mother carried her grief with her, and hadn't completely mourned Israel's death yet, but several months later, still in Japan, Amy was born. I had a sister to love and adore. Amy was tiny, perfect, and beautiful. I just wanted to watch her, talk to her, and protect her. I thought she was the most remarkable thing I had ever seen. I didn't realize I could love someone as much as I loved my mommy and daddy, but I did.

3
IN TORNADO LAND

Of all places, after living in Japan, we moved to Topeka, Kansas, in the middle of the country and cornfields. My dad had a psychiatric residency at the renowned Menninger Institute there. Soon after this move, Mom was to suffer another terrible loss when her young mother died of ovarian cancer, foreshadowing a big chapter to come.

It was 1966. Between the deaths of my brother and grandmother, my mom was overwhelmed with sadness and anger. For a while, I felt I had lost my mother and, to a degree, my father. Dad was working long hours in his residency, then moonlighting for extra money for the family. My mom was physically there, but it felt like she was mentally absent and couldn't tolerate me. I don't think my mom had the mental space to tolerate much of anything.

As children, our imaginations are often consciously very active, but our ability to differentiate between fantasy and reality are still being formed. At that time, I imagined I had pushed my parents away, that I had caused their pain. Despite only having small pieces of memory from this period, I carried with me a profound sadness, loss, and personal insecurity that I would not understand for many years. It also took time and work for my mom to grieve and come to terms with not only her mother's death, but also Israel's.

In spite of all this, I tended to be a resilient little girl, and continued to be very curious and outgoing, especially where babies and birth were concerned. A neighbor was pregnant with her fourth child, and I was again fascinated by her noticeable roundness and the waddle in her walk.

Dougie, her older son, was my age, and we would often play together.

I recall asking my parents one day, "Is Dougie's mommy's tummy that big because there's a baby in there?"

I received a simple, matter-of-fact "Yes" from Mommy, as Daddy smiled, looking on.

Of course, being six now, I had many more words than I'd had when I was two and three. I asked how the baby would get out when it seemed to be so big. I knew at this point that it had to come out of the vagina, but I just couldn't figure out how. My parents explained as they always did, without jargon and always using anatomically correct language.

"Dougie's mommy will push the baby out of her vagina, which will stretch and get big enough for the baby."

"Will it hurt?" I asked.

My mother answered, "No, it doesn't hurt. It feels like you are pushing out a very big defecation."

I remember thinking this was amazing. I wanted to know what it would be like to 'defecate' a baby out someday. I wondered if Dougie knew what was in his mommy's tummy and if he knew how this was all going to play out.

I ran next door to find Dougie already playing outside. I was so excited. I ran up to him asking the question at hand. Of course, he knew there was a baby in his mommy's tummy, and a stork would be delivering it soon.

"A stork? I don't think so." I considered for a minute. "That's silly. It's in your mommy's tummy, so she has to bring it, not a stork. She has to push it out her vagina, like defecating." He was far from interested—in fact, he was insulted and emphatically furious. Before I could register his anger, Dougie had cocked his fist and popped me in the face! I was burning with pain and humiliation. I was stunned! I ran home crying, and my mother and father explained to me that not all parents are comfortable talking so openly with their children. This was very difficult for me to understand, as my parents also had talked with me about how important honesty is, and yet this exception to the rule seemed pretty huge. Even though Dougie hit me, I started to learn about empathy and that friendship is nuanced by the way we speak to each other. These were early seeds being planted in my mind that led me to become a therapist many years later.

There was one other incident with Dougie that influenced my view of the world and my love of people and life. One day, not long after the last incident, Dougie and I were playing together. He accused me of using a bad word. He said I better be nice and use only good words or I could get my mouth washed out with soap. I had no idea what he was talking about. He explained that when he used 'bad words' or said 'bad things,' his parents would make him eat soap. He said it was terrible, and he would cry. I could hardly believe what he was saying. I didn't even know what a 'bad word' was.

He explained, "You know…like 'vagina.' Or 'fuck,' or 'sixty-nine'…"

I ran back home and asked my parents if they would ever wash *my* mouth out with soap. They seemed to startle and look a little shocked, wondering what had given me such an idea. In my family ideals, sexuality and physiology were never reacted to with shock or punishment, but violence or cruelty were always taken very seriously, and I think this classified as both.

I simply answered, "Dougie."

My mother and father explained that they did not believe children or anyone should be forced to eat soap or have their mouths washed out with it.

"It is not good for you or a very nice thing to do to anyone, especially a child," they told me.

I thoroughly agreed, and was relieved.

I still wanted to know what the two new 'bad words' meant. In my memory, my parents were sincere and thoughtful in their explanations, but as they have since told me, they were pretty amused. They explained that there is no such thing as a 'bad' word.

"'Fuck' is a word some people use to describe how mommies and daddies make babies when they love each other very much," they said. "And sometimes, when mommies and daddies love each other very much and kiss each other all over, daddies can kiss a mommy's vagina and mommies can kiss a daddy's penis. When they do it at the same time, they make the shape of a six and a nine. Those two numbers snuggled together are sixty-nine."

And what did I think of that? "Oh," I said, only mildly impressed. "Okay."

It wasn't a big deal. What *was* a big deal was the shock I felt about parents who would wash their children's mouths out with soap. I believe this was another pivotal moment in my mind. An idea was growing within me. I wanted to help people to not be mean to each other and to understand that there is no such thing as a bad word. What a world it would be if we could all understand that it's not the words we use that are bad, but how we use them.

II

GOOD UNTIL I WASN'T
—LOST REBEL

"Endure and persist;
this pain will turn to good by and by."
—Ovid (43 BCE-17 CE)
Roman Poet

4
STILL GOOD

I was excited when we moved to Los Angeles in 1966, where I would spend most of my growing-up years. My father had finished his psychiatric residency, and one of his older brothers, Ted, thought my dad would love the west coast. Uncle Ted invited us to visit him at his home in Malibu and take a look. I remember being entranced and frightened by my first sight of the ocean in his backyard. He and my aunt Barbara lovingly held my hands and walked me slowly to the water's edge. I was so worried that if my new pants got wet from the seawater my mother would be mad at me. They had such an easy-breezy way about them. They laughed and tenderly assured me it would be okay. That was the beginning of my love affair with the ocean and California.

Although we didn't live on the beach, we eventually moved to a house in Santa Monica that was only blocks away. My dad started his private practice as a psychoanalyst in Beverly Hills, and Mom had her hands full with Amy and me. It was there, in 1969, that my youngest sister, Laura, was born. I was fascinated and deeply in love. I loved holding Laura, rocking her, making up songs for her, changing her diapers, and more than anything, watching her nurse.

Her head was so teeny, and my mother's breasts seemed so large and bountiful. My sister's face would turn bright red, almost purple, as she sucked. She seemed to be over-the-moon milk-drunk. Now that I was a big nine-year-old, my mom explained that when she had given birth to me, not many women breastfed their babies because they were embarrassed. I wanted to know why, but she didn't know why. Now, nine years later, it had become much more acceptable, and people were more open.

After all, 1969 in Los Angeles was the heyday of the "make love, not war," "flower-power," "our bodies are beautiful" generation—thank God, for me and my sisters. We benefited from having intellectual parents who were loving, affectionate, and open to the cultural influences of their time. The defining influence boiled down to love.

By the time I started middle school, I had been in two nursery schools and three different elementary schools, corresponding with each geographical move my parents made. This transience, on top of previous unconscious memories that registered in me as feelings of insecurity and sadness when introduced to new situations, left me very fearful and resistant to starting at another new school. The issue was that starting anything "new" also meant finishing and saying goodbye to something familiar. This felt like a loss or death, like the death of my brother or grandmother—the grief of which was yet undigested. I only knew I felt a heart-wrenching dread when I started something new.

5
MIDDLE SCHOOL LOOMS —LIKE MIDDLE EARTH

I had skipped fourth grade, and was placed in a fifth-grade class.

"This is Briar Flicker, who is skipping fourth grade this year," my teacher said, introducing me to the class. "I do not believe in skipping, but here she is. This will be a tough year, young lady, and don't expect any special treatment. You may sit in the back of the class."

So began yet another dreaded "transition," but it seemed that this time my dread might have been well-founded. That year was hell, and the following year was only marginally better, although I did make friends and at least felt socially included. When I learned that my next school would consist of 3,000 kids—1,000 in my class—and was told by older kids that us seventh-graders would be teased mercilessly, I was struck with terror. There was *no way* I was going to *that* school!

Maybe there is a God, because shortly after learning about the seemingly gigantic local middle school that should have been my destiny, I was saved! Praise all things lucky! My sister's best friend's mom, Rhoda, was starting a new school, and it was to have only a seventh and eighth grade that first year with approximately thirty kids to begin with. The plan was that each year a new grade would be added with another fifteen kids each. This felt like an even playing field. We would all meet and start together at the same time.

It turned out there were thirty-three of us that first year with three main teachers: John, Art, and our headmistress, Rhoda, who also taught our science classes. We were encouraged to call our teachers by their first names, which felt like an incredible honor, and we learned with them, played with them, and fought with them. It really was an extraordinary learning experience on every level, one which I wish more young people could have. I think we would have many more creative and well-adjusted adults if parents collaborated regularly with their children on learning and attended to their developmental needs.

I was one of the founding students of The Crossroads School For Arts and Sciences. I definitely loved the arts more than the sciences. I loved literature, acting, the humanities, languages, dancing—folk, modern, anything dancey they would throw at me—and even the fine art classes. One of the required classes every year was "Community Service," and I loved that, too. I loved reading to the elderly in nursing homes and listening to their amazing stories—I mean, who was contributing to whom?

Crossroads and my family laid an important foundation with me that inspired my love of learning and people. I don't think I ever lost these completely, but they definitely faltered during a period to come. The process of becoming the best we can be is a roundabout path that involves pain, loss, frustration, and sorrow as much as love and good times.

6
INKLINGS OF TROUBLE...
LITTLE TEEN, LITTLE TROUBLES;
BIG TEEN, BIG TROUBLES

S eventh and eighth grade were years I found my sea legs at Crossroads. I had my best friends, but I still hadn't had a "boyfriend,"
which some of my friends had. In eighth grade—awfully young—
one of my closest friends "lost her virginity" with a boy we thought was
one of the cutest in school—good thing we had our priorities straight.
I worked hard at my academics, but felt increasingly distracted and resistant to it, fine-tuning my procrastination skills. The barometer of my
internal world was beginning to experience adolescent warping.

One of our ongoing assignments in school was to keep a journal. An
adult might think that this was a wonderful practice for us, with all
our growing pains and adjustments to our ever-morphing psyche-
somas. It wasn't for me. We were to write in the journal every day for
thirty minutes using a free-flow of thoughts, and it was to be "private."
Despite assurances of privacy, we were expected to turn in our journals
every week. My best friend and I didn't understand why our teachers
needed our journals if they were going to remain private. Who wants

to pour their deepest thoughts and feelings out in a journal when you suspect that your privacy will be invaded?

My friend and I decided we would "challenge the system" and write a "Curse-Word Dictionary." It would be every derogatory and bawdy word that we could think of. It was silly and defiant, tween acting-out at its best. We would sit together and define "ass," "bitch," "bastard," "fart," and old favorites like "fuck" and "sixty-nine." Some words were tamer and some were hard-core, aimed at getting a rise out of our teachers, who were not supposed to be reading our submissions. I felt like I was pushing the limits despite what my parents had told me years earlier, that there were no 'bad' words. There might not be 'bad' words, but truly, my intentions were to shock the teachers who said they weren't reading our private journals and confront their hypocrisy. I thought they would be shocked and angry, and then I could be indignant that they had lied about reading the journals and perhaps change the system.

As you might have guessed, the teachers *were* reading our journals, and my friend and I were called in to discuss our content. Surprisingly, the teachers weren't "mad"; it was much worse. They were "disappointed." They wanted us to learn to use writing in a new way that might benefit us for the rest of our lives—but that was too lofty for me at twelve years old. At that time, the only thing I heard was that they had betrayed my trust and read what they said would be private. If they hadn't broken my trust, maybe I could have truly begun to explore my inner thoughts and feelings, trusting they were for me alone to consider and ponder, and developed an invaluable lifetime habit way back then.

Today, keeping a journal has become an indispensable part of my life for personal and business development. I think my friend and I were not the only ones to challenge the journaling assignment, because soon after the humiliating conversation with my teachers, the assignment was dropped. I like to think that maybe the teachers had learned something, too.

7

CURIOSITY, KISSES, AND CATASTROPHE

T he little rebel in me was getting bigger and bolder. I had increasingly more time to myself, less parental supervision, and enough space to swing out and try my wings. Between seventh and eighth grade, my sisters and I went for our first time to stay with my grandparents in Miami Beach, Florida, while my parents took a much-needed vacation to Acapulco. My grandparents' house was right on the bay. In the beginning, Grandma would walk my sisters and me to one of the local hotels where we could access the beach and hang out for the day. I wanted to stay all day and meet kids my age, long after Grandma and my sisters were done. Reluctantly, Grandma and Grandpa let me.

I was a kid from California, and in Florida, that was pretty cool. I was a little bratty and braggy about how the waves at "my beach" were so much better than the little ripples of the Atlantic in Miami. I was actually surprised when the Florida kids were impressed with my stories of 'ginormous' waves and the dangers of body surfing I had encountered, fully embellished with jelly-fish stings and near-drownings. I found it felt good to be "sort of" known, showing only what I wanted to show, scared to be seen as a geeky little girl who was still trying to find her social spot back at home in the 'real world.'

That first year in Miami, when I was twelve, I met a boy at the beach who seemed to like me. He was visiting from New York for the week. He had sort of a tough-guy accent, yet he seemed sweet and interested in me. We danced in the teen disco, swam and splashed for hours in the ocean, and occasionally held hands or touched each other playfully, flirting. One day, as he was walking me back to meet my Grandma to be picked up from the beach, we stopped and looked at each other. The ocean was shimmering on one side of us and cars were speeding by on the main road on the other side. It was the sweetly cliché moment I had dreamed of. I was going to have my first kiss *on the beach*.

He moved in slowly and—bam. He kissed me—long and with tongue. I had heard about this tongue thing—French kissing—but really wasn't sure how common it was and hadn't thought it would happen to me. It was wet, wonderful, and very surprising. He left for home that evening with his parents, never to cross my path again. I cried and listened to sad music, but I was in heaven.

The following summer, I met Joe not far from where my parents first met each other. He was my first real true boyfriend, the first boy I loved. He was a couple years older than me, smart, kind, a 'surfer.' He often talked about how next summer he would be sixteen and able to drive us on dates. I was very impressed. There were movie dates, deep probing conversations about life, love, and school, long walks and swims at the beach, and even a kiss or two that summer. I couldn't wait to share my photographs and stories back home with my friends. Joe and I wrote to each other all year, and I would date him a few times the following summer. We soon realized, though, that it just wasn't the same as it had been the year before. We cried together, broke up, and that was that.

It seemed to me that with first kisses and infatuation, the door opened for all kinds of curiosity and mischief. At the start of eighth grade, I was aware that there were a number of kids throughout the school who had tried smoking pot. These were kids who were considered the popular ones. During the prior year, following a "drug education class," I had feared that smoking marijuana could lead directly to heroin addiction, but by now I had seen enough to know that wasn't true. I figured if it was offered, I might just try it. I might try it and not tell my parents—another little something new.

Up until this point, I had been very open and forthcoming with my parents with everything. But now, as a young teenager, I was getting stirrings of wanting to differentiate and separate myself from my parents. It wasn't due to a concern about getting in trouble that I didn't want to tell my parents. They were very open to talking about anything and everything. On the contrary, it was me who was starting to feel proprietary and possessive of some of my experiences. I was starting to think about whether or not I could try things out, rebel, and discover without sharing everything with my parents.

This cute boy I had noticed on day one of the new school year was handsome, seemed funny and comfortable in his skin, and lived within walking distance of my house. One day after school, he invited me to walk with him to the beach. We lived a few blocks from Lifeguard Station 18—my hangout for years. As we walked to the beach, this boy took out a joint and asked if I had ever smoked before. I told him I had not ever tried pot, but admitted I was curious. He lit the joint nonchalantly and told me I probably wouldn't feel any effect this first time, but next time I probably would. I felt my heart pounding with nervousness, but I was going to play it cool. I coughed and sputtered after my first couple hits, but I liked the boy, and I liked that this might be an easy way to get in with the popular kids. The popular kids were not the ones who were the happiest, most morally driven, or intellectually motivated—but they were smoking cigarettes, pot, and hashish, and were sexually precocious. I thought I wanted to be like them, and if I was, I would live happily ever after. If smoking pot was part of being cool, I decided I would smoke pot the next chance I got as well. The boy was right; the joint had no effect on me that first time.

My life over the next few years was accentuated by many firsts. I smoked my first cigarette when my best friend stole a couple from her parents. One night when my parents were out and we were home alone, we went through my dad's closet and found a cigar box. Curious, we opened it and found a secret treasure: a 'rolling machine' for rolling marijuana cigarettes. There was a little film canister that was three-quarters full of pot, and a little tin-foil packet which hid a tiny nugget of hash. Then the most unique treasure of all: a tiny hash pipe. This was not an ordinary pipe. My friend and I realized with giggles that the pipe was shaped like a little penis that stood upright by balancing on its testicles. You drew on the pipe by sucking on the penis.

Over a period of months, my friend and I would pilfer a little of my dad's stash here and there. I didn't realize at the time that it was never depleted by anyone other than me. For my parents, it was something they had around for entertaining, like wine and alcohol.

I was completely stunned when, one night at dinner, my father asked very casually why it was that I had been stealing from him.

"Stealing?" I asked, mortified.

"Yes," he answered, "I noticed the other night that my marijuana and hashish were almost all gone. I don't suppose either of your sisters have been taking it."

Again with the proper words. It was so hard to appreciate, at that time, my mother and father's frankness with me and willingness to address issues straight on. I was angry and embarrassed.

I kept my mouth shut and just didn't respond, and I definitely wasn't going to cop to taking their drugs. I was angry that I couldn't just take their stash, and I knew it was wrong, but I was also, on some level, relieved that my dad was letting me know that he had his eyes on me. The punishment was baring the burden of my parents' disappointment in me. In that moment, we didn't get into a discussion about drugs. The bigger issue was my stealing and secrecy. The amount of marijuana they were talking about was less than a quarter ounce over a six-month period. At that point, the pot wasn't what concerned them; it was helping me develop a healthy conscience.

I never went into their stash again, but I did venture into growing my own pot. That didn't go well either. I grew my marijuana in pots on our rooftop. It was where I thought no one ever went or would see. The plants were filling in and flowering, and I was proud of how well my horticultural experiment was going. The next thing I knew, it had all disappeared. My mom played it off at another family dinner. This time, she and Dad did not take the direct approach, but their meaning was clear: they had their antennae up and on me. Mom said she had noticed "weeds" growing on our roof and asked the gardener to get rid of them. I was furious and trapped. If I got angry outwardly, it was tantamount to admitting that I had overstepped their boundaries and broken the law. I chose to pretend I didn't know what she was talking about, and my guilt, embarrassment, and anger were awful.

I want to emphasize that during the '70s smoking pot was very trendy, avant-garde. Although I think my dad might have taken a hit or two in a social situation, he preferred a fine wine. My mom was not interested in pot, but again, would be a host ready for her guests. It was such a different time. As for me, my parents had two concerns: 1) As a fourteen-year-old, why did I feel the need to alter my reality? But this wasn't their greater concern. They didn't see experimenting with pot as much different from their experimenting with alcohol at a similar age. 2) They were much more concerned that I was being sneaky. They were teaching me that they could be indirect or gentle and yet crystal clear. You don't need to yell at a child whose conscience can be overly active and harsh, and such was the case with me. I heard them loud and clear. I do believe that today, and in today's culture, they might have handled the situation differently, but I think they were really trying to understand what was underneath this shift in my behavior—which had always been so open.

I was quite the adventurer, and put myself in danger a few times with unsavory characters and unsavory drugs. Always, my saving grace was the love and sturdiness of my parents. If I went too far, they knew that grounding me for a week (or month, or two) brought me back to earth.

At the height of my adolescent testing and boundary-pushing, I got permission to borrow my mom's brand-new, beloved Toyota Celica. I grabbed my guitar, bought a six-pack of beer at the local liquor store (passing for twenty-one at seventeen), picked up one of my best friends, and off we headed to the clothing-optional beach at Topanga. We had been there only a few minutes, singing and drinking, when some guys came over with their guitars to join us. We shared our beers, and they shared some quaaludes. Quaaludes were also known as "horse tranquilizers," and for good reason. They were very, very strong, and should never be consumed with alcohol.

They let us know that they had a studio up in Topanga Canyon not far from the beach. They said we should go with them and do some recording. Sure, that makes a ton of sense. Let's drive somewhere remote with boys we don't know, stoned out of our minds. The only sensible decision I was able to make was that I should not be driving. I knew if I drove I would die. Instead, I got into a car with a couple of boys we just met. My friend drove my mom's car, taking one of the other boys who knew the way.

I left a few minutes after my friend did. The road in Topanga Canyon is a curvy, narrow, wild ride in the best of times, and this was not the best of times. Around a curve we came, ten minutes into the drive, and there was my mom's car, in a ditch. My friend's face had hit the windshield, and the glass was one big shattered spiderweb. The boy with her was fine, but her nose was broken. He and the boys I was with in the other car explained they had to go pretty damn quick, since they had outstanding warrants for traffic violations. I suspected there might be various and sundry other offenses they were in violation of. Off they went, leaving me and girlfriend at the side of the road, stoned and a little drunk with her broken face!

We had no cell phones back then, but we did have an extraordinary amount of sobering fear. A fire truck found us within the hour and called a tow truck, but we were left to navigate our way home on our own. How did we get home? We did what any nice young girls in 1976 would do: we hitchhiked, of course. It's kind of crazy that I survived my teen years.

That was probably the worst incident of my adolescence, but I have to admit there were others. My family jokes to this day that I would probably still be grounded if I hadn't gone off and gotten married, but I'm getting ahead of myself.

Through all my experimentation and rowdiness, my mom had a pretty decent barometer for sensing if I was in real trouble or just into annoying kid stuff. By this time, not only was my father a psychoanalyst, but my mother was in psychoanalytic training at an institute focused on child development. Together they were an awe-inspiring, formidable power-couple. There were times I wanted to hate them, but I just couldn't. Mom and Dad definitely picked their battles with me, always coming back to how much they loved me. This was the secret power they were bestowing on me: the knowledge that love always wins. As long as my grades were good and I had good friendships, they didn't worry too much. They were *mostly* hands off, eyes open. But that doesn't mean they didn't set boundaries and enforce the rules. When I broke my word or didn't keep our agreements, like if I came home after curfew, they did not hesitate to provide limits and boundaries and ground me or suspend certain privileges. This was done out of profound love.

As I discuss with parents today who come to me for coaching or therapy, teens need to figure out how to separate from their beloved parents before going off on their own. It's often not easy. It feels easier to be furious and leave people you're angry with than to admit to needing and loving them for their help and attention.

8
GETTING BANGED UP CATCHES UP

I was becoming increasingly boy crazy. I seemed to have to have a boyfriend in order to validate and feel good about myself. I didn't feel I was able to love myself enough to stand strong on my own. My boyfriends were a stand-in for my self-confidence.

I had a "boyfriend" in ninth grade whom I'd met skiing. He was an Adonis—his strong, athletic body, long blond hair, and tender soul took my breath away. One week, he had a school break when I still had class, and my parents allowed him to visit. He rode his bike sixty miles to come see me. He made me feel so magically loved and so grown-up. Sometimes, feeling 'grown-up' is a sure sign you aren't.

We did love our romance. The kissing and heavy petting, the sweetness of our first sexual exploration—everything in every which way except intercourse. I felt like nothing could bring me down. Living so far apart, however, going to different schools, and being so young, our romance was short lived.

In tenth grade, Michael entered my life. A bruised boy, only a little older than me, dark, romantic, introduced to the world of sexuality by an older waitress; he seduced me with his passion and prowess. Again, I was both flattered and infatuated. I borrowed my sense of self and security from him. It seemed wonderful.

My junior year, after Michael moved away to Northern California, I met a handsome musician who attended a nearby alternative school. I think I was enamored by the way he played his guitar and the seductive way he looked at me. But he was more troubled and more broken than anyone I had met. He also liked me less, but I was infatuated and turned on. He was the typical bad boy whose rugged look and tremendous musical talent lured me in. We would spend hours playing guitar and singing, but he just wasn't particularly nice. He wasn't mean, but he was all about his music. Looking back, I think I was hoping for true love, but he saw me as merely a mutually talented friend with benefits. After an uneventful loss of my virginity, I moved on yet again.

In an awful and strange way, I believe I was trying to save these guys I came across, to compensate for the loss of my little brother so many years earlier. I hadn't been able to save Israel, but I would save other lost struggling boys. Despite the love and openness with which I had been raised, what was now catching up was very old guilt and grief that had never been worked through. During this time of growth, when young people are getting ready to launch into their adulthood, often the unfinished business of early childhood will resurface. For me, I was looking to resurrect my little brother, Israel. If I could help a wounded or 'bad' boy, unconsciously I felt I would absolve myself of the guilt I mistakenly carried that Israel's death was my fault.

During the summer between junior and senior year of high school, when I was sixteen, I attended a college program at the University of California at Santa Barbara and met a great guy, who I would be with for two years. He was not dark or broken, but golden and creative. We felt a mutual worship of and infatuation with each other. He wrote poetry for me in books he hand-bound. We explored art, history, philosophy, and nature together. We explored each other's bodies and minds in ways that were new and different. I believe that during the two years we spent together I was able to appreciate and adore the ways in which this young man reminded me of the best of my family, and I brought him my openness, love, and tenderness. I think that there was a brief window of time in which we joined up, challenged each other, and related in ways that I wanted but wasn't mature enough to accept. I still hadn't dealt with my personal insecurity and infantile guilt. In college, by our second year together, because he was so lovely, good, and giving, I felt claustrophobic. In my immaturity and insecurity, I ran.

When I began college, on the surface, life was great. I could not believe I had been accepted to the University of California at Santa Cruz (UCSC). I was even lucky enough to be accepted to Stirling University in Scotland for my junior year as a study abroad. Sex, drugs, and rock and roll shaped the contours of my college life—laced with some study time now and then. If my parents had been there, they would have known I was getting into deeper emotional trouble based on the poor quality of my friendships and the dismissive attitude I had about my academics. Although I was making friends, they were not going to be my forever friends like the kids at Crossroads, who I still have close relationships with and who mean the world to me.

One of my biggest problems throughout college was that I would forsake deepening the possibility of real friendships for the fantasy that having a boyfriend would make me whole and complete. I was not alone at college for long. I soon met an angry, sultry, over-indulgent, unmotivated, and entitled 'older' man. He was twenty-six and had returned to college to complete his degree in English. He seemed encyclopedic in his knowledge of rock and roll and loved music that I hadn't heard of. He seemed full of all sorts of interesting experiences that smacked of both rebellion and art. We would stay together until after we graduated with a brief hiatus while I was in Scotland.

It didn't dawn on me that my need to have intense relationships with young men in order to feel more whole was a reflection of my own brokenness. Often, we don't realize that the only way to claim our sense of worth and value is to do so from within, through self-exploration and development. I thought I came off as so cool and together, while inside I felt fragile and frightened of really growing up and feeling good enough.

Much of my college experience is a blur because I was afraid to face anything head-on. I lacked a sturdy sense of self, commitment, focus, and maturity. To offset my inner chaos, I acted out in mind-altering ways by experimenting with psilocybin mushrooms, LSD, pot, hash, pills, booze, coke, and sex. I was in trouble, and no one knew to reach out to me. I was quietly devolving, but from an outside view, I think I looked like I was in pretty good shape. I performed, produced, and directed plays, was liked by teachers, and completed the curriculum for a double major for a Bachelor of Arts in theater and literature in four years. I didn't exactly fit the profile of a depressed underachiever.

When I spent my year in Scotland, I did discover inklings of what it was to stand on my own, by being so far from home and in another culture. I left my boyfriend behind, and with him a lot of limiting behavior. I worked hard, enjoyed life, and loved my new friend Hilary and the other girls in the dorm. They opened their hearts to me, despite my often bad behavior (especially if a boy showed up). I learned so much about my personal and academic self that year. I became interested in the history, art, and music of the United Kingdom and was able to take some unforgettable classes, particularly on J.R.R. Tolkien. Hilary and I traveled in Europe and skied in the Italian Alps. I was in a Stirling University production of *Cabaret*. My experiences and relationships were transformative.

When I graduated from Santa Cruz the following year, I reattached myself to my old boyfriend, even though I knew he wasn't good for me. I felt light, alive, and curious during that year in Scotland, but not when I was back with this guy. Nonetheless, he and I moved to Los Angeles and got an apartment. I worked hard and was trying to find my place in the world. I was waiting tables in restaurants, serving cocktails, singing, and playing my guitar in bars. I put together my headshots, but never went on a single audition.

I did go to my uncle Ted's house weekly for mentoring, where he infused me with his opinions at our routine lunch. Being a director and writer in Hollywood for many years, and the person who had first taken me into the ocean, I idealized him. I also believe that he often spoke to me on behalf of my parents as they were all quite close. Uncle Ted had the belief that I was too soft to pursue an acting career. He said I would be gobbled up and spit out, and I believed him. Belief is 99 percent of the fuel we require for any accomplishment, and I was running low on belief in myself. I may have had the talent, but my self-confidence and self-esteem had been eroding for years.

One of the jobs I liked at the time was managing an art gallery in Century City. I even started taking some business classes because the interest had been sparked in me. I was making some real money for the first time in my life and was so excited—but when I shared with my boyfriend all that I was learning and doing at the end of the day, he would ask me why I was trying to make him feel like such shit. He felt I was waving my success in his face. I felt worse and worse, and, worst of all, I felt ashamed to talk to anyone about what was really happening with me.

One day, I was invited to brunch at the home of my parents' best friends. My boyfriend did not want to go with me, feeling he would be ostracized because he had been unemployed for so long. Over dessert and tea, I broke down and started to cry. I unburdened myself of all the pretenses I had been living with. I shared about how much this man's contempt for me was tearing me apart. And this was made worse by the fact that he was smoking huge amounts of pot, drinking excessively, and not working. I had become very bored and disinterested with all mind-altering substances at this point and was beginning to really want more for myself. Everyone was so shockingly understanding and kind. They were patient and interested and wanted to hear everything. They *really* wanted to hear everything.

In my mind, I felt that I had so defiled myself and forsaken my values. I could not have imagined my family understanding and continuing to love me. I "knew" at this point I *really* was a bad person.

I may have learned young that there are no bad words, but I clearly hadn't learned I was not a bad person. That day was the beginning of my return to my 'self' and discovering my real value.

By the end of brunch, having talked and cried myself out, my parents and their friends helped me realize I needed to move back in with my parents and sort myself out. I was still irrationally terrified that my boyfriend wouldn't "let" me leave, but my parents went with me to my apartment to help me pack and ensure I got out unscathed. I think my fear was more related to a crazy guilt I felt for leaving. And when I showed up to take my things, although this man was very sad and hurt, he was also uncharacteristically sober and made no move to hold me back.

III

THE TURNAROUND

*"Success is not final; failure is not fatal.
It is the courage to continue that counts."*
-WINSTON CHURCHILL (1874-1965)
BRITISH POLITICIAN, ARMY OFFICER, WRITER, AND PRIME MINISTER OF THE
UNITED KINGDOM WHO LED BRITAIN TO VICTORY IN WORLD WAR II

9
GETTING HELP AND FAILING FORWARD

So there I was, weeping in the bedroom I had grown up in, rocking in the old rocking chair my mother had nursed me on as a baby. I felt so lost and like a complete failure. My mom must have heard me because she came in and sat down. I told her how alone and lonely I felt, and that, ultimately, how I felt my self-worth was very much connected to whether or not I had a boyfriend. I could see that this wasn't right. I could see that I "should" feel good about myself just because I knew I was a good person, but on an emotional level, some part of me felt profoundly sad and 'bad.' I recognized that having recently graduated from college and having been discouraged by family and my own internal critics from pursuing a career in acting, I had no idea of what I wanted to do with my life professionally. I didn't realize that I was in the boat with a ton of other new graduates who all faced similar questions. I thought it was a reflection of what a loser I uniquely was.

My mom listened and listened. She looked thoughtful and full of love for me. After a pause, my mom suggested a few things that forever altered my approach to hardship and pain. She didn't tell me to stop crying, she didn't ridicule me as I ridiculed myself in my mind, but she did tell me that if I was sad I should put a time limit on how long I would allow myself to wallow in my pain. I remember laughing when she told me I should allow myself a solid ten to twenty minutes to really enjoy wallowing. It made me laugh, because I felt so understood. Wallowing sounded wonderful, like a mud bath up to my neck in self-indulgence. And here she was telling me I was *allowed* to wallow and that she even encouraged it.

The next thing my mom wanted me to consider was starting an analysis, as in psychoanalysis. Having grown up with parents who were analysts, I knew what this implied. She was talking about lying on a couch four to five times a week to do an archeological exploration of my mind. In psychoanalysis, "mind" refers to the experience anyone has of their intellect and emotions, as well as how the two coexist together both consciously and unconsciously. When our thoughts and feelings are out of sync with each other, we can have difficulty experiencing happiness. I felt intrigued and hopeful, but also fearful about what I might have been hiding from myself.

Last of all, my mom suggested we talk about this at dinner as a family, where my parents would listen and help me, not punish me. Even my little sisters listened with love, concern, and perhaps shock that their big sister, who seemed so accomplished, felt like such a loser.

My parents referred me to one of my father's teachers, Dr. Albert Mason. I am forever indebted to him. Many years later, he was to become one of my favorite instructors and clinical supervisors when I started training as a psychoanalyst. On his couch, I learned to be in contact with the "baby part" of myself and trust his sensitive, attuned listening. I finally began to discover language for the feelings I had carried with me since the deaths of my little brother and grandmother. I had been too young to be consciously aware of what I was going through at the time. Dr. Mason helped me track my dreams, and free-flow of thoughts, and fantasies (otherwise known as "free associations"). Tenderly but sturdily, Dr. Mason helped me excavate the buried regions of my mind.

Through tears of sadness, fear, and rage, I discovered the guilt I carried with me through my infantile imaginings that it was my fault Israel died. I must emphasize that this was discovered through long, hard, deep work. I led the way by saying whatever came to mind, as best as I could, without editing. I shared very raw thoughts, feelings, and dreams. Sometimes my sessions were full of silence. I came to understand how important and full of meaning silences were. It was in silence that I fell in love with myself.

10
PERCHANCE TO DREAM—
AND THEN TO UNDERSTAND

There were two important dreams I had, among many, that stand out as very meaningful representations of how dream work helped me. Early in my psychoanalysis, I had a nightmare that I had cancer. In the dream, I watched as a single surgeon opened my stomach to remove the cancer that was killing me. I was very frightened of dying and of the surgery and couldn't decide which was worse. As I told Dr. Mason about the dream, he wondered with me if maybe this dream represented a 'me' who was afraid of our working together. Might I think of him as the surgeon who might have to cut me open to find cancerous thoughts and feelings buried deep inside? I was afraid of what was inside me, and that what was in my mind could be deadly. I was equally afraid of getting it out, even though I thought it might help.

Finally, through our work on this dream, Dr. Mason helped me to understand that our dreams have multiple levels of meaning. Our dreams can tell a story, represent influences from our waking life, or represent different aspects of oneself. Through this nightmare of cancer, I began to be able to think about my conflicting feelings that were scaring me. The 'doctor-me' wanted to move forward, look inside, and heal me, and the 'patient-me' was fearful and scared of losing everything because I felt I was 'rotten' from the inside out.

A couple years later, I dreamed of a multitiered garden. It was beautiful, full of all sorts of flowers. It filled all my senses; I could smell the lovely fragrances, feel a cool breeze, see every color in the rainbow, vibrant and beautiful. I still remember not wanting to wake up from this dream. I wanted to explore every level, one beautiful tier at a time. This dream was so different in feeling from the first one, yet the subject was similar. As soon as I shared it with Dr. Mason, I realized "many-tiered" was an unconscious play on the idea of being "many-teared." What had felt unconsciously cancerous in my dreamworld was not truly cancer, but was the only way I could hold experiences incomprehensible to a child. Over time, these memories so terrible inside of me registered as what killed my grandmother: cancer.

As my first analysis was coming toward its conclusion, I was able to turn my pain and tears into a blossoming. The lower tiers/tears were for my brother; the upper tiers/tears encompassed not only my grandmother's death, but the death of a childhood friend who had been like a brother to me, the death of my paternal grandfather who I adored, and the death of my first dog, Bascomb. As I became able to grieve these losses, I also became able to feel more creative and confident. In this dream, I was able to conjure an image of a beautiful, internal, world-garden that represented my mind: full of beauty and blossoming, but also able to contain my many tears.

11
VENTURING OUT AND FINDING MY WAY

While I was undergoing my analysis, I began to take my growth and development on the road and venture out in life. I also wasn't interested, at that time, in dating. I discovered that instead I just wanted to come to know myself better.

One day, I went out to lunch with one of my best friends from Crossroads. We were struggling, new college graduates wondering what was next. I had gotten tired of waiting tables and was now managing the gallery in Century City, but I felt really tepid about it all. I had been completely put off of acting at this point.

My friend was one of the smartest people I knew, so I was surprised to hear how dissatisfied she felt. She had been working with young boys in a residential treatment center, and it was painful to see the boys' parents undermining them—if they *had* parents. It was even more awful to see seven- and eight-year-olds who had already been bounced from foster home to group home and weren't wanted anywhere. The more she spoke, the more I felt moved. Maybe I could help kids like this. It fit into my trajectory of loving children and babies. I could use my interest in the service of helping children in need, and make a salary to boot.

I was nervous, having never "studied" psychology, that I wouldn't be able to enter the field. My studies in acting and literature were actually great courses in psychology, but I didn't know that then. I drove to several local residential treatment centers to submit my resume, such that it was, and request interviews. One called me back for an interview: The Florence Crittenton Center for Young Women. I was thrilled. As a result of that interview, I was invited to be a full-time counselor who would work with one of the social workers as her junior partner. Unfortunately, like many residential treatment centers across the country, this one closed many years ago due to lack of funding, but it turned out to be a life-altering and unique experience for which I am forever grateful.

There were four groups of girls in this home, a total of forty residents divided on two floors of a beautiful old Victorian mansion. The girls ranged in age from twelve to eighteen. The girls on the second floor were pregnant or had babies. The girls on the third floor had "failed" at foster care, having been bounced from home to home, in juvenile hall, involved with gang bangers, or had been hospitalized. One girl I remember was sixteen and had lied about her age when she was arrested. She was placed in Sybil Brand, a prison for adults, for six months before they realized she was a minor and transferred her to Crittenton.

My girls were the third-floor "hard-asses." I was responsible for knowing where they were at all times, making sure they showed up at meal time, and that they went to school. I took them shopping for clothes and out to the movies. I made sure they went to bed when they were supposed to. I also was given the opportunity to co-lead therapy groups with the social worker who hired me. She clearly cared deeply for these kids and was very bright, warm, and a generous teacher to me. We ran two groups a week with our girls, and they each had individual therapy as well. I was able to sit in on some sessions with certain girls, and at one point when the house was very full, I was asked to pick up some slack and see some of the girls individually on an as-needed basis.

Turns out I was pretty good at defusing high tension in the house, a talent I discovered along the way out of necessity. The professional childcare workers who had been at Florence Crittenton for years called me The Kid From West of La Brea, meaning outright that I was a soft, rich, white girl. They were implying I'd never make it in this tough house in this tough neighborhood. They were wrong. I loved it there. My coworkers and the kids taught me a lot in the two years I was there. I learned my strengths and weaknesses, grew my sense of humor, and gained a broader view of the world.

I know the exact moment where my sense of humor and courage grew exponentially. The first time I ever took "my girls" out shopping was also at the very beginning of my time at Crittenton. Another staff person was going to "ride along" for the purpose of supervising and supporting me if I needed it. I had recently received my Class 3 driver's license, which allowed me to drive our oversized van. It is an understatement to say I was a little nervous, both about driving and about supervising these ten rebellious teens.

The first sign that this was going to be a tough day was when one of the girls shoved her way from the back of the van to the front so that she could adjust the radio station and volume to listen to her sexually evocative music. This girl, who I will call Sue, stood 5'11" and weighed approximately 250 pounds. The bright orange afro pick wedged in her hair sparkled with the hair oil she drenched herself in to keep her Jheri-curl shiny. On the outside, she was big and tough and literally threw her weight around on our first field trip together. The other girls egged her on. My coworker said nothing, so, quivering inside a little bit, neither did I. We went to a mall to shop at JC Penney. I naively asked the girls how it worked for them with other counselors, and they claimed they just went off on their own and would meet me back at a prearranged check-out counter in an hour to pay for everything. Fine. Again, my counterpart said nothing. A couple of girls who were new to Crittenton stayed close to me, so I took the opportunity to get to know them better and help them shop for blue jeans, T-shirts, and pajamas. I began to relax and found that I was having some fun with them.

Meeting up with everyone was uneventful, and some of the girls were even eager to show me their selections. I was especially surprised when Sue approached me, smiling and excited about finding a pair of flannel flowered pajamas that came with a stuffed bear. Suddenly this big, tough, scary girl transformed, and I saw her as she must have been as a very young child. She was looking for approval and love, just like the rest of us.

With everything paid for, the girls started warming up to me a bit and let their guards down. They wanted to go for a walk on Sunset Boulevard. I didn't think that was the best plan, but, again, my passive and quiet cohort gave me no input or guidance, just a shrug and a nod. I was uncomfortable from the minute we arrived.

Most of the girls showed up at the time we had all agreed to, except for three. The girls who did show up were helpful in retracing their friends' steps. Just as I started to feel hopeless and panicky, trying to figure out if I should call the police or the home first, I saw the three missing girls happy and chatting as they casually approached the van. I thought I would faint with the rush of relief I felt. Trying to keep my composure and remain calm, I asked the girls why they were so late and if they were okay.

"Oh yeah, we're great," they replied. "We did a questionnaire at the Scientology place, and then saw we've gotta go! We're late, damn! Whatever…"

I was speechless. I had no idea what to make of their comments, cavalier attitude, or lateness.

There was something so bizarre about the whole night. I was dumbstruck that I had been entrusted with these really tough kids without training, without instruction, and with a partner who seemed to be not at all affected or engaged by anything that happened that night. In this state of puzzlement, I got in the van, and was relieved to be heading back to Crittenton. I was wondering if I really did have the bones to undertake this new challenge or if I had made a mistake.

As I was lost in thought and wishing that the night was over already, another girl jettisoned herself at the radio and this time cranked the catchy beat up deafeningly loud. We were on the freeway, minutes away from the home. The girls started singing at the top of their lungs and rocking in unison. They rocked back and forth with such strength that the whole van started to rock, too. Now my thoughts were flying at breakneck speeds as I considered that if we crashed and only suffered from broken necks as a result, that would be a good outcome compared to the alternative I pictured, that we might all die instantly as I lost control of the van, causing a massive pileup on the road. What was I going to do? When I turned the music down, they'd "get in my face" and turn it up. When I told them they needed to settle down, they'd say, "Or what, bitch?" and rock more fiercely. I was driving twenty-five miles per hour, thinking we were going to roll. Clearly, I did not have their respect or partnership, and yet only moments earlier I had felt we'd made progress in connecting and getting along. It was only later that I came to understand that as a result of tremendous abuse and neglect, the road to forming warm, trusting relationships would be defined by two steps forward, one step back, over a very long haul. Proving oneself to be trustworthy wouldn't happen in one evening, let alone one interaction.

With cars and sixteen-wheelers negotiating the curvy Hollywood freeway at full speed all around me, I decided to step on the brakes. In lane number two, I came to a full stop.

One girl called out, "What the fuck are you doing, nigger?"

I put the car in park and turned around to address her respectfully and authentically. I simply said that I was stopping.

Another girl said, "You gonna get us all killed!"

I said that that might be so, but I would rather die by oncoming traffic than by speeding along with my ears bleeding, getting seasick with rocking that would make us roll and kill us anyway. If we die, I explained, it's going to be my way. Not theirs. I turned the music off and looked each one in their eyes. My coworker remained silent, but his face had gone pale. I stared him down, too. I felt bad for the girls, but I was infuriated with my "partner." I believe that this all occurred in less than a minute, but time moved slowly. In the instant I stopped the van, I felt calm and able to think. I evenly announced that when everyone had taken their seats, buckled in, and shut their mouths, I would continue on. I turned back to the road with my hands on the steering wheel, waiting for compliance. I heard a series of clicks. It took maybe two seconds. There was silence as I put the car into gear and drove back to the house.

When we got back to Crittenton, some of the girls were very quiet, looking at me as they passed by. I think they were wondering if I was batshit crazy. The other girls seemed outright grateful that I had been able to contain their peers' kooky antics and hugged me before going up to their rooms.

I had to remain past my clock-out time to complete an "incident report" and talk with the house supervisors. I let them know I was sorry for how out of control the evening had gotten and that if they wanted to fire me I would understand. I also said that I thought it had been bad judgment to send me out as a new counselor without real guidance, training, and/ or support. I was honest and detailed about what had happened, blow by blow. As I reported, my supervisors, who had little more training than I had, as I was to learn later, were grinning and nodding. Apparently I had gone through a rite of initiation and passed with flying colors. I was also to learn that others had experienced similar beginnings, but that mine would go down in Crittenton history. Slapping my palm on my face, shaking my head, I thought, *Great.*

I came to realize that this night had been very valuable. I recognized my ability to think on my feet and saw that I would never be bullied or allow others in my care to be hurt without putting up a damn good fight. I saw that I had a capacity to see beauty and vulnerability under tough exteriors, even when I felt threatened. I saw that my love for people outweighed my fear. I saw that I had internalized the values and ethics my parents had hoped to instill in me, despite the wandering I had done, and that I would never again fear to speak my mind.

Between my work at Crittenton and my self-work in psychoanalysis, I was coming to really value myself and feel sturdy as a human being.

I was wandering through my thoughts and feelings one day on the couch in my analysis, and it occurred to me that I was hungry to know more about psychology. Despite having two parents who were analysts, I only took one psychology class in college. I always felt a deep love and curiosity toward people, but I was unconsciously fearful of acknowledging it academically. I felt as if I would lose my own individual identity if I took a psychology class and morphed into my parents. I imagined I couldn't be me and approach the same field of interest my parents were in and still maintain my me-ness. During these years at Crittenton and in psychoanalysis, I found my desire to learn and deepen my knowledge about the mind, people, and psychology growing. I wound up taking classes at my local city college. I took an introductory course followed by developmental, physiological, and abnormal psychology, and loved them.

At the same time, I was doing more on my own. Along with my analysis, I had started reading books on self-development and personal growth. I was discovering myself from many vantage points. I was smart, sturdy, independent, and good enough. I decided I was ready to take the Graduate Record Exam (GRE) and start applying to graduate school programs for social work and psychology. I would be grateful to go into whatever program would take me. This would be my next chapter.

IV

MAGIC MOMENTS

"For man, as for flower and beast and bird, the supreme triumph is to be most vividly, most perfectly alive."
—D. H. LAWRENCE (1885-1930)
ENGLISH AUTHOR, PLAYWRIGHT, POET, AND JOURNALIST

12
FINDING ME

I was very worried about whether or not I would get into any graduate program in psychology or social work given my academic history, but theater and literature were not so different from psychology or sociology. All of them require an understanding of character and relationships. To my great surprise, I was accepted to every social work program I applied to, and a couple Ph.D. programs in psychology. My younger sister, Amy, had graduated from her undergraduate program and was applying to graduate schools during this same period as me. She also applied for social work school, and we both got into New York University's School of Social Work.

The potential to study with Amy was the deal clincher. I accepted the invitation to join the social work program at NYU. I was a little nervous and sad to be ending my analysis with Dr. Mason but also thrilled to be taking my next steps; moving to New York, living with my sister, and getting to know my New York family better.

13
ROCKING MY WORLD

I loved school and living with my sister. When we arrived in New York, we stayed with one of our uncles and his family for a few days. He and my aunt had lived in the city for most of their lives, in an already-crowded but very cozy apartment in Stuyvesant Town with their three young children. It was hilarious having seven of us in their two-bedroom place.

Our uncle and aunt walked the Manhattan avenues with us, getting us oriented to "The City." One day, we did a practice run of getting to Washington Square where the Social Work School was, and then back to where our apartment would be. It felt like we were living in a grown-up, urban wonderland. I was no longer interested in artificially altering my consciousness; I had developed instead my self-confidence, and with it an ability to experience greater curiosity, awareness, and pleasure in all of my relationships and in my connection with reality. It now felt great, not fearful, to go out as a family. Amy and I began to spend time together, too, developing our adult friendship and sisterhood.

The day came when we were able to check into our apartment on the ninth floor of a brand-new Manhattan high-rise. We each had our own fully furnished room and shared a common area with a small dining table and two chairs. We had a view that looked out at nothing but a nondescript building across the street—no romantic view of the Empire State Building or Central Park. We were in one of the few personality-less neighborhoods of New York City: 26th Street between 1st and 2nd. Our claim to fame was that we were a block away from Bellevue Hospital, infamous in old movies for its creepy, locked wards for the insane. We had a kitchen that was so tiny that if you took a single step in any direction you were no longer in the kitchen. We were thrilled, and it felt perfect. We were ready to begin our new adventure.

Classes started up, and we received our clinical assignments. My sister was going to work with autistic children downtown, and I was going to work on inpatient psychiatry in a ward with adults in the Bronx. We were learning, making friends, and eating lots of fabulous pizza and Chinese noodles, which fit perfectly into our restricted student budgets.

Having moved to New York from Los Angeles, I did experience some grief over not being able to go to my daily aerobics class with Richard Simmons. It had become another form of therapy and personal development that I loved and highly valued. I looked for some classes at NYU and some of the local gyms but was very disappointed. After all, who is going to stand up to Richard in his short shorts, flamboyant outfits, and grueling classes?

I discovered that across from the laundry room in the basement of my apartment building was a large "multi-purpose" room that wasn't being used for anything. I decided I would start my own aerobics classes and bring Simmons's teaching style to the residents of student housing. I received permission to use the space daily, and they even put in floor-to-ceiling mirrors for me. All I needed was my boombox and tape mixes and we were good to go.

It wasn't long before my aerobics classes were packed. I became friendly with many of my students and found it was a great way to meet people, make friends, and occasionally even get a date. Even though I wasn't looking for a serious relationship, it was great to go out on dates and catch a movie, dinner, or an opera with interesting people. Every aspect of my life felt fulfilled.

My goal was to graduate and go back to Los Angeles to start my professional life, working with people to help make the world a better place, one life at a time. My dream, triggered by my work at Florence Crittenton, was that I could express my passion for life by helping others discover theirs.

That said, an old Yiddish adage comes to mind: "People plan and God laughs." I had made friends with a young woman in my aerobics class, and we would often either go out or back to my place to hang out after class. We never went to her place. She had a crush on her roommate, a "nice Jewish boy from Long Island" who was studying dentistry, and she explained, half-joking, that if he and I met we would fall in love and get married, dashing her chances forever.

I was only too happy to clarify that I had no interest in meeting a nice boy from Long Island. Besides, when I was at school in Scotland, I had received a sentimental letter from my dad that contained all sorts of life advice. My dad, in his infinite wisdom, encouraged me to fully explore life's options, but also to take some care in the department of love. When the time to settle down came, the only profession to beware of was...*dentistry*. "Because," explained my dad, "dentists do the same tedious things day in and day out. Their procedures are limited and repetitive, and make them dull."

The final warning was that dentists have the highest rate of suicide. His message was that when I was ready, I should find someone as lively, curious, smart, and adventurous as me. I was convinced. I would have no interest in a 'dentist-to-be.' In addition to Dad's warning, dentists hurt you, even if it's for a 'good' reason. I could never fall in love with someone whose leading trait seemed to be sadism.

It was the new year, and my family took our annual trip to Beaver Creek, Colorado. Every time I got to the top of the mountain, the mountains called to me like a Siren song. Had I not discovered a love for helping others as a psychotherapist, I might have pursued becoming a ski instructor and retired to the Rocky Mountains forever.

That first week back in New York, my new friend with the dental student roommate approached me after aerobics. She missed me and wondered if I wanted to come over. She thought we could bring in sushi and get caught up. After having known her for a year and having never gone back to her place, I was a little dumbstruck. She said that Jay, the dentist, had to study for a test in "root canals"—gross—and he would be out until late. She wanted me to bring my photos from skiing, and she'd get the food. I thought that was a great trade.

Later that evening, we were laughing, enjoying our meal, and drinking a little wine. I spread out photos of snow-covered slopes and family shots. We were having a great time. Suddenly, I noticed the front door jolt open. Jay's hands must have been full with "root canal" books, so when he unlocked the front door, he used his body weight to push it open. It flew with a bang into the inner apartment wall. As he got his balance, almost falling over, he saw my friend and me. He seemed to go all white, back out of the door for a minute as though he had made an egregious mistake, and seemed to be checking the apartment number. Once he saw that he was indeed where he belonged, he re-entered with a newfound confidence and definite balance.

"Hi, I'm Briar," I said.

"I know," he said. "I'm Jay, and it's so nice to meet you."

He did not look like the "old guy" nerdy dentists I pictured in my imagination. He was very handsome with his sparkly, mischievous hazel eyes, expressive full lips, wavy hair the color of honey, and a pronounced dimple smack dab in the middle of his chin. We became chatty and comfortable immediately. My friend went a little pale.

Jay was going to go skiing for the first time the next day with some friends, and he had come home early to pack. He wasn't sure about what to bring and, as if we had known each other for years, I followed him into his room to help him pack. The whole time we kept up a light banter, and both of us commented on how funny it was that I had just gotten back from my own ski trip. Before the night was over, Jay asked if he could give me a call when he got back from his trip. Still a little surprised to have my dinner and social time with my friend interrupted and then end up with this flirtation, without much thought about his being of the "forbidden" profession, I said, "Sure."

Our poor friend was not so happy about how the evening turned out, despite putting on a good face. It took time and conversation to work it all out as the relationship between Jay and me unfolded.

14
B'SHERET—DESTINY

W hat I didn't know was that Jay had been stalking me for months. I suppose that's how our mutual friend developed her hypothesis that if we met, we'd fall in love. She knew that Jay was already intrigued and smitten. I believe that this is also why she encouraged me, ultimately, to go out with him, knowing that they truly were just roommates.

It just so happened that one day, when Jay had to go down to the basement to do his laundry, he felt the walls thumping rhythmically and heard my dulcet tones barking out orders to my aerobics class. Jay's friend, the Rastafarian janitor in our building, happened to be sweeping up right then, so Jay grabbed him, left his clothes as they gyrated to "spin cycle," and walked across the hall to see if I might be gyrating as well.

They found their ideal viewing spot, where Jay, loving the whole *Flashdance* look of "underwear worn on the outside," as he says, saw me for the first time and was allegedly stricken by the sight of me. He asked his friend if he knew me.

"Sure," he said. "I know her; that's Briar, mon."

Jay asked, "What's a briarmon?"

He replied, "No, mon, that's Briar...mon!"

"Oh, Briar! That's Briar—her name is Briar!"

For months, Jay strategized. He found himself doing his laundry whenever I taught my class. I later asked him why he just watched my class and never actually came to take it. He told me that he had a terrifying fantasy that he would come to class and be very excited about the opportunity to actually meet me, but that as soon as we started working out, it would be too hard for him, and, completely overcome by exhaustion, he would humiliate himself by passing out. He thought that once he fainted in the middle of my class I would never give him the time of day. However, once he found me on his turf, literally in his living room, he felt that nothing would stop him from pursuing me.

In the Chasidic Jewish tradition, there is a tale about love based on the idea of b'sheret. B'sheret actually means destiny. In the old folk tradition, the story is that God splits every soul before it is born. Each person then seeks, in life, to be rejoined with the mate from whom they were separated at birth. In this way, we reunify our souls and become spiritually complete. I am not a religious person, but am a big fan of romance, and I definitely identify with a good ethnic folk tale. From our first meeting onward, I came to enjoy the notion that Jay and I finding each other was b'sheret. From our first date on, our time together was easy, interesting, and buzzing with passion.

Our first date was interesting because, again, Jay had a big test coming up, and he didn't have a lot of time to spare. What he didn't tell me was that before taking me out to dinner that evening, he was bringing another girl he was dating to the same restaurant first. Jay was young and just didn't think it through. All he could manage was figuring out the logistics to fit everything in, while not really accounting for the underlying issues quite yet. The restaurant was only a block away from our apartments, so it was really fast, easy, inexpensive, great food and great service. He took his first date to Chang's Chinese Restaurant, his local favorite, brought her home, and told her he would be back later after he was done studying. He then took me to Chang's.

We had one delicious course after another, paired with good beer, and finished up with traditional plum wine. Our conversation didn't miss a beat, and I felt like I had known Jay for years. He was interested in my passion for people and desire to help others. He had studied psychology as a minor at the State University of New York at Albany with a major in computer programming, two areas that he felt would be important to his practice of dentistry in the future. He believed that the future of dentistry and business would necessitate an understanding of computers, and that technology would be significant in the future world. Remember, small home computers were a new phenomenon back then. I thought his conceptualization for his professional future was really visionary and insightful.

He told me how he had known that he'd wanted to be a dentist since he was ten years old because he loved people's smiles. He loved that he could be a doctor who helped people, but unlike his uncle, who was a cardiologist, he would never have to deal with patient fatalities. He didn't want to have patients who died. I could completely identify with that. This dentist didn't seem boring or sadistic at all.

After dinner, Jay walked me back to my apartment. I was already anticipating having him come in and spend a little more time with me. I opened the door, and before much of anything else could transpire, he told me he had to go finish studying for a test but that he would call me. He leaned in for a kiss. I was hoping for something slow, passionate, and drawn out. But no. I was shocked. A quick, dry, closed-mouth peck, and he was off. It was so quick, in fact, that when I realized the kiss was over, and I dreamily opened my eyes, he was already halfway down the corridor. I thought maybe Jay was a little sadistic, after all.

He had been funny, but also able to talk about politics, philosophy, and his personal life and upbringing. I was physically attracted to him. He was also clearly interested in me and curious about everything I had to say. It felt so easy with Jay from the start. By our second date, I had the oddest, most wonderful feeling that I had met my b'sheret.

15
LOVE WITH FREEDOM AND EASE

Love always requires work, but it is the kiss of death when a relationship is tense and problematic from the beginning, when love isn't able to take root, and fighting is destructive, not constructive. What I have consistently seen throughout my professional and personal experience is that when love is mature and healthy, it isn't inordinately difficult.

Jay and I went on our second date only a few days later. We sat together for hours eating, drinking, and getting to know each other. We talked about our life dreams and goals, who and how we wanted to help, financial aspirations, children, religion, education, and where we each had imagined settling to build our lives. It was magical, but at the same time the most *real* conversation I'd ever had with a man I'd liked.

He also told me then that he hadn't been altogether truthful on our first date. He told me he had been dating a girl, and that he hadn't been fair to her or me. He explained the reason he had run out on me on our first date was that he made the date with me so impulsively he didn't realize he'd had another date that same night with someone he wasn't crazy about. He had worried about being rude to the first girl, but also didn't want to give up his time with me.

It seemed to me Jay was sweating up a storm, he was so nervous and felt so guilty. It was clear he didn't want to hurt anyone, and he seemed very cute and vulnerable, expecting a tongue-lashing. It also felt like he thought he wasn't supposed to be dating other people. The fact of the matter was that although I wasn't looking for a serious relationship in New York, I was *also* dating other people. I thought it was pretty funny and burst into laughter. It was clear he had struggled with this incident, and mine was not the reaction he had expected. I told Jay that I had been dating other people as well, and that I wasn't eager to get overly involved with anyone in New York. I basically told him we could have fun for a few months, but after graduation, I was eager to build my life on the West Coast. I think we were both amused by how similarly easy-going our reactions to each other were, and it was equally exciting to discover a kindred sense of humor. We knew we had an undeniable connection that was probably meant to be forever, but there was no admitting that yet, to each other or to ourselves. We plan, and God laughs.

Within a couple months, we found ourselves carrying a queen-size futon on the subway from the lower east side back to my apartment. We must have been a sight, but we didn't mind—we were not squishing one more night. The romance of the "cozy" single bed was fleeting, and I loved Jay's ability to be romantic *and* pragmatic.

Jay still had his own place, but we never slept alone again. Just prior to shopping for our new mattress, Jay and I had a life-changing conversation while snuggling on the old mattress. Our conversations had been wonderful, and so was the sex. Making love was an adventure in tenderness, passion, and fulfillment. Everything we enjoyed about our conversations was expressed in parallel when we had sex: the openness, humor, willingness to explore, kindness, passion, and tension. I knew on a preconscious level that I really could spend the rest of my life with Jay.

On one particularly lazy afternoon, as we lay cuddling in the afterglow of adoring each other from head to toe, Jay suddenly propped himself up on top of me, looked me in the eyes, and told me he had something important to ask me. I thought, *Oh no, don't ruin this.* Everything was going so well.

"We are obviously enjoying ourselves and spending a lot of time together," he began. "This relationship could go one of two ways. We could keep it light and fun and keep going the way we are without any other commitments, and keep dating the other people who are in our lives, or…we could let those other people know that we are in a serious relationship now and not dating anyone else."

In my head, I was thinking that Jay was crazy. After all, we had only been dating a couple months. How could I possibly get serious with this guy from New York? I had a plan. I was going to graduate and go home, and he still had training to do in New York. I couldn't possibly be in an exclusive relationship right now.

That was my head. My heart said something else altogether.

Before my head could intervene, my heart took over, and I told Jay I loved him. "I'm in. Let's give this a try."

I couldn't believe that that's what fell out of my mouth. It was a week or so later that I found myself hoisting an oversized, overweight futon onto the subway with the man that I would spend the rest of my life with.

16
THE SPERM DONOR DINNER

I thought I had become a pragmatist as a result of my analysis, and that I had become strategic about love. Although in some regards that might be true, I still ultimately trusted in romance and intuition, just like my parents had. I was pretty well grounded and able to stand firm, but still full of curiosity, love, and an adventurous spirit.

Shortly after agreeing to an exclusive relationship, Jay took me out to dinner at a very elegant and pricey restaurant. I often paid for meals when we went out back then, because, as a social work student, my schedule allowed me to hold down a lucrative job at a bustling restaurant in the Village. Jay, on the other hand, had a schedule in dental school that barely gave him time to breathe let alone make an income. We kept dinners out to a minimum, and when we did go out, we were limited by a shoestring budget.

On this particular night, knowing that Jay had every intention of treating me, I asked him point blank, "How are you even affording this?"

As we sipped Bombay martinis and savored escargot, Jay looked a little uncomfortable and surprised with my question. He usually seemed at ease in our conversations, and this just wasn't his style. My curiosity was even more piqued.

"I'm thrilled you are enjoying the meal," he began, "because I just got paid today for a recent job I took. A recruiter came to the dental school a month or two ago looking for students who might be interested in becoming sperm donors. The recruiter said that donors were badly needed for infertile couples, and they would pay me generously."

There was a pause. Yet again, I fell in love with him a little more. I found his worry over telling me so endearing and comical. It was not something Jay anticipated I would understand. He expected I would relate to him as a strict, prudish, critical, and jealous mother figure. I sensed that this conversation felt to him like he was crossing a boundary of indecent exposure from which we as a couple might not recover. He was so very wrong.

Again, love just isn't meant to be difficult. This interaction was another example of how easy our connection was and how, in the face of worry about being accepted and understood, jumping in and being honest led to a better, deeper relationship! We had no way of knowing then how important this conversation would prove to be in the future. Then, all we knew was that we were building a relationship on a foundation of openness and honesty, a bit of good humor, and with a spirit of generosity and love that would forever flavor our relationship.

17
SPRING BREAK

Everything was moving so fast. It felt like I had only just arrived in New York, then all of a sudden, I was getting ready to graduate with my Master of Social Work, deeply in love with Jay.

Spring break, 1986, was when I first brought Jay home to California. I let my parents know that I thought I was seriously in love. I think the intensity of my feelings had grown and was transmitted to my parents loud and clear in a way they'd never heard from me before. We spoke about how quickly our relationship was growing and why. My parents were eager to meet Jay.

Then my mom explained that my youngest sister was in my old room with her boyfriend. She wondered if I could stay in my sister's room. I literally felt blood surge to my face. No way. I would have *my* room. I decorated and furnished it with my earnings from Crittenton, and my sixteen-year-old baby sister was not going to kick me out because she wanted the comfort of my room with the queen-sized bed rather than the single bed in her room to suit her romantic needs when her little boyfriend was over (Sibling rivalry much?). I admit my reaction was over the top, but Jay and I were still living in crappy NYU housing. *I* wanted to come home to the comfort of my room, with the comfort of my big bed, in the comfort of the arms of my amazing guy. I argued all of this with my parents on the phone. Jay was listening in and hitting me on the arm. He couldn't believe that I was telling my parents about how I wanted my bed so that I could sleep with him under their roof. He was nothing short of mortified as he listened in. Again, I was amused. He knew that I had an open relationship with my parents, but hearing this conversation highlighted how real it was. When we talked seriously about it afterward, he noticed that despite feeling embarrassed, he was also inspired and eager to meet my mom and dad. Love, laugh, and 'be,' I always say.

Jay knew that my parents were both analysts, and that made him a little worried. Jay grilled me on the plane.

"Are they going to analyze everything I say?"

"Well…what do you mean by 'analyze'?" I asked. "Do you mean judge and criticize?"

"Maybe," he said.

"They are going to love you! You are warm and smart and caring and funny! What are you worried about?"

He, of course, worried that they wouldn't like him, and that they would be critical because I had announced unequivocally to them that we were sexually active, that I liked my sex with him, and that I wanted my sister out of my room so we could enjoy ourselves in it. He felt the whole thing was already so awkward, and he hadn't even met my mom and dad.

"What if I'm just quiet?" he wondered.

"Well," I suggested, feeling a little sadistic and very entertained watching him grapple with his needless anxiety, "if you're quiet, they'll just analyze the silence."

I laughed hard, then mustered my compassion and empathy to remind him of how much I loved him. Being an analyst or therapist means being understanding and interested. "Analyzing" is not criticizing; it's engaging in thinking and communicating together.

I told him my parents were eager to meet him. We'd probably go out for lunch when we landed to someplace fabulous, then go back to the house and relax and get to know each other. He definitely breathed a little easier, but he made me promise that until he got acquainted with my parents a bit, that I wouldn't leave him alone with them. I agreed.

18
MEET THE FLICKERS, PART II

One of the first things Jay would learn about the Flicker family was that we travel prepared but compact. Whether we are gone for a week or a month, we never check luggage on a plane because we only bring a roll-on bag and a tote. That's it. This makes for easy departure, arrival, and getting around wherever we may be. This was a refreshing change for Jay.

My parents were waiting for us curbside when we landed. I quickly introduced Jay to my parents as we climbed into the car and zoomed off to The Ivy at the Shore. The Ivy at the Shore, still delicious today and in the same location, was an airy California-Americana Nouveau eatery, with floor-to-ceiling windows, summery flower arrangements, white linen tablecloths, and servers who were mostly aspiring actors of the beautiful people variety.

"Hi, I'm John, and I'll be your server today." The server's introduction was often worth the price of admission.

As I had found from my first meeting with Jay, his conversation was easy and free-roaming with my parents. My mom and dad also happen to be experts at setting people at ease, naturally exuding love and friendly curiosity, and this was true with Jay, too.

Jay talked about his interest in dentistry. He shared his dreams of making sure people had smiles they loved and mouths that were healthy. He expressed his heartfelt belief that smiling with pride and dignity supports self-esteem and confidence overall. He described the medical training he'd received in his first year of dental school and how it had been no different than the training general medical doctors received in their initial year. I noticed my dad's eyes lighting up throughout the conversation as he connected with Jay's story and passion. I think my dad would have loved it if one of my sisters or I had pursued a medical career, and he felt an immediate 'click' with Jay. We discussed politics, travel, religion, and what we had planned for this week-long visit. I think my parents marveled at how much Jay could eat, and when we were all fed, full, and the bill was paid, we made our way home.

When we got to Casa Flicker, Dad and Jay were deep in conversation, leading the way. My mom and I were gabbing, not really cognizant that the guys went straight through the entry hall to the kitchen and then out back to the pool. My mom and I exited stage right to my bedroom to drop off luggage and catch up for only a minute or two. I had been distracted, and I completely forgot about my promise to Jay to stay by his side.

Unbeknownst to me, while Mom and I caught up, my dad invited Jay to step outside and have a glass of chardonnay and, "By the way, would you like to go in the hot tub?"

"Sure, sounds amazing," Jay said, unsuspecting of what was to come next.

My dad peeled off his clothes, and standing stark naked, said, "C'mon, I've been heating the water."

Oooh, this was something that I really hadn't gotten to discuss with Jay yet. One of the other quirky aspects of my California upbringing was the comfort that my parents had imparted to me and my sisters about our bodies. We grew up knowing that we all have bodies and that they can be different sizes, shapes, and colors, and that we should never be ashamed of who we are or the bodies we live in. We didn't walk around the house naked, per se, but if we were going in the hot tub, sauna, or pool, you wouldn't find my parents or me suited up. And so, there was Jay with my dad, who was completely naked within hours of their having met each other. Jay wondered first where the hell I was, then whether or not my dad was testing him somehow. Jay considered what my dad would think if he declined to undress and wouldn't just jump in with him, and then what my dad would think if he did undress. These thoughts flew through his mind in nanoseconds, and in an instant, before he could overthink it, his clothes were off and he was in the tub with dear old Dad.

Meanwhile, I had a panicky moment when I realized that my mom and I had been in my room talking for quite some time, and I remembered my promise to Jay. Oh no! I suspected that my dad would be great with Jay, but I didn't know how Jay would feel with me out of sight. I told my mom I had to go check on Jay and dashed out of my room where she was helping me unpack. I peeked in the living room. No Jay. I looked in the kitchen. Empty. I glanced out a window in the kitchen, into the backyard, and there they were. I swallowed, took a breath, and braced myself as I dashed out the back door.

"Hey," I called out, trying to seem casual and unconcerned. "How's it going?"

Jay looked at me helplessly, shaking his head but smiling. He tilted his wine glass toward me, implying that life was actually treating him well despite some initial shock. Dad responded for both of them. "We are having a wonderful time, honey. Jay was just telling me about his gap year in Israel. What a great experience that must have been."

My dad was absolutely jovial, at ease, and in his element. Jay seemed to get right back into his conversation with my dad without missing a beat, laughing and diving back into their discussion. Like clockwork, at the same time, my mom came outside to check in, and before we knew it, my dad was asking my mom and me to join them in the hot tub. I cannot begin to tell you what shade of red Jay's face went. I roar with laughter every time I think of it. It was awkward enough initially for Jay to be naked in the water with my dad, but he was going to lose it if my mom started to take her clothes off and get in with them. Before another word could be said, or article of clothing removed, I suggested that Mom and I needed to prepare some food for dinner and they should just enjoy each other and their time together privately. Later that evening, Jay didn't know if he wanted to hug me or hit me. Thankfully, hugging won out.

The rest of that trip went seamlessly. Jay met more of my family, we took walks on the beach, we went to Beverly Hills to shop, and I gave him a tour of my parents' offices, where I hoped to work soon. We saw a few movies, and he met some of my friends. He loved everyone he met and was loved by everyone who met him. By the end of the trip, Jay understood why I was eager to return to my family, friends, and sunny, laid-back lifestyle.

19
LOVE AND MARRIAGE

We returned to New York, rejuvenated and relieved from our Flicker follies. I'm not clear whether it was in spite of the hot tub incident or maybe because of it that my affection and love for Jay was stronger than ever. I was starting to feel conflicted as the end of the school year crept closer. I would graduate soon, and had had every intention of leaving New York. Would Jay and I have a long-distance relationship? Would we say goodbye and be grateful for the time we had spent together? I was having thoughts and feelings that left me unsettled and truly upset. I was having a tough time thinking it all through.

It was less than six months into our relationship, but it felt like we had known each other for a lifetime. I was completely up in the air about where we might go next. On a beautiful Manhattan spring day, Jay asked if I would be open to moving out of our graduate student apartments to get a "real" place in the city with him.

"You are asking me to stay, after I graduate?" I asked, stunned.

I had whispers of feeling that we might be headed toward marriage, but I did not want to give up on my dream to settle in Los Angeles. I was also clear that, having lived with my college boyfriend, I didn't want to "play house" again. Despite not having taken marriage vows, the "move-out" had been horrific and terribly painful, and I had decided that, in the future, I would not live with another man unless we were married or altar-bound.

I shared my feelings with Jay. Jay smiled and gave me a mischievous hazel-eyed wink. "What if you knew that by the end of summer you would have a ring on your finger?"

At the time, I felt like he was only reassuring me that he was serious and that a proposal was on its way. But now I also see that he was unsure about my desires, and he was testing to see where I leaned in our relationship. If I moved in with him, he would know that I loved him unconditionally, and he indirectly would have the answer to his unproposed proposal. My answer in that moment would make our next step clear. It was all in my court.

That June, after a festive graduation ceremony—all the more thrilling because I had the privilege of receiving my master's degree hand in hand with my sister—Jay and I moved into our first home together. We found a duplex on the upper east side, butted up against a cheese-and-olive shop. Our apartment had a wrought-iron spiral staircase and a main wall of exposed brick. Our dining area and living room ended in a sliding glass door and opened to our own little back garden. This was a gem in New York and felt practically palatial. Living next to the cheese shop also had its obvious perks, until one day Jay let out a shriek—sure enough, we had mice. Not long after that, we adopted a cat from the nearby animal shelter, a rocky mountain coon cat we called Sigmund. I got my first job working as a therapist for adolescent girls at Hawthorne Cedar Knolls Residential Treatment Center. Our home was perfect, and my job was great. Life was really good.

My parents, family, and friends were happy I was staying on with Jay and that we were so happy. There are never guarantees from moment to moment in any life, but I was riding a wonderful wave and believed with all my heart I would have been foolish and cowardly to let my preconceived plans override the evidence of my experience. And so I stayed, and continued to nurture and trust in my relationship with Jay and launch my career as a novice therapist in New York.

My life seemed to lurch forward at hyper-speed, back then. We moved into our first apartment in June. In July, Jay invited me to join him in his parents' home in Long Island to celebrate his mother's fiftieth birthday. He said he had some other fun plans in store as well. I was game; I looked forward to a little getaway out of the city. Jay's mom's party was to be a Sunday brunch, so he made plans for us on Saturday evening to go to an outdoor modern dance performance and picnic. Unfortunately, the weather was non-compliant. The sky dumped buckets of rain. There were spiderwebs of lightning and soul-rattling thunder all afternoon and evening. Our event for the evening was a wash. I was disappointed, but Jay had a contingency plan.

"Let's go see *Aliens*, then we can go grab a bite."

It was not exactly the romantic evening I had been looking forward to, but at least there was still the possibility of a good thrill—and we would be together.

It was a typically sticky humid East Coast summer night, relieved a little by the rain. We dressed as comfortably as we could and headed out in his family's old station wagon. We held hands during the movie, and Sigourney Weaver did not disappoint. I screamed out loud, gasped a half a dozen times, and found myself almost in Jay's lap by the end of the movie. Afterward, Jay still wanted a picnic, but it continued to pour, and I vetoed the plan.

"We can pick something up and find a romantic spot to watch the rain fall while we eat together in the car, all nice and cozy," he said.

I thought this sounded anything but cozy—more like claustrophobic.

I countered sweetly, "Let's go out some place for Italian maybe, where there are tables and candles and waiters."

"No," he answered slowly as if he was thinking about it. His reluctance became apparent, but I didn't know why it felt like this was becoming a big deal. I was beginning to get annoyed. I couldn't understand why he did not want to go out to a nice dry, air-conditioned, candle-lit little bistro and salvage the rest of the evening.

After some discussion, I was feeling sulky. My mood didn't improve when we pulled into a parking lot where the only open eatery was a fast food chain specializing in inedible roast beef. I generally have never been a big fast food fan, and my interest in consuming overcooked, unrecognizable "meat substance" on an oversized white-bread bun was somewhere around nil. In fact, I thought maybe Jay was joking.

This was no joke. Jay put the car in park after a brief disagreement and marched up to the counter. I stayed in the car, feeling the steam build up in my head. I was pissed off and wanted to explode, and not for any logical reason. Sometimes reason is overrated. Poor Jay came back to the car with two loaded roast beef specials—gross. Mustard and ketchup on the beef—super gross. Two diet cokes—how romantic.

As we drove along the highway to somewhere unbeknownst to me, the rain stopped beating down, the view outside became crystal clear, and Jay pushed play on a Crosby, Stills, Nash & Young cassette tape. I started to feel a little better—then guilty about being shrewish and blowing the experience of the evening way out of proportion.

We arrived at Jones Beach, and there wasn't another human being to be seen. We ambled over to the boardwalk and started to stroll together in the quiet with our arms around each other. Everything felt clean and crisp from the earlier rain. There was a partial moon reflecting on the ocean, and the waves were still stirred up and powerful from the storm. After a few minutes, I stopped and took Jay's face in my hands.

"I'm so sorry I have been so bitchy tonight," I said. "It isn't your fault. I was aggravated, but I know you just wanted me to have a nice evening out and there wasn't much to choose from. I love you, and I love that we are here at the beach. You are a good, good man, Dr. Jay."

Jay still had one more year of dental school before he was officially "Dr. Anything," but I had stumbled upon the nickname, and it stuck. I felt moved and touched by Jay's efforts and love for me. He was clearly moved, too, because he seemed to wobble and fell to one knee. His eyes glittered, and I felt his love and adoration as he looked at me, but it didn't occur to me why he was on one knee. Was he okay?

Jay told me he never imagined meeting someone that he would ever feel so loved by or feel so much love for. He couldn't believe that I was apologizing when it really had been a challenging afternoon and evening. That's part of why he loved me.

"I can't imagine living my life without you," he said. "I cannot imagine ever waking up and not finding you by my side. You inspire me and bring extraordinary joy to my life, and all I ever want to do is make you happy."

He reached into his pocket and pulled out a little iconic jewelry box.

As he opened it, he asked, "Will you please spend your life with me, forever? Will you please marry me and be my wife?"

I couldn't peel my eyes away from his gaze. It was like the whole world vanished for the moment and only we existed. I could sort of acknowledge and take in what was happening, but it felt surreal. It wasn't totally unexpected, but at the same time it was a complete surprise. I felt tears well up in my eyes and my body involuntarily jump into Jay's arms. "Yes," I cried. "I would be honored to be your wife." I had no doubt.

This is how it was with Jay. Even when we disagreed or had difficult issues to discuss, we got to it, worked it through, and the hugging and kissing would resume.

After I accepted his proposal, we found our way to a phone booth on the boardwalk. Jay nervously shoved quarters into the phone and called my parents to get their approval of our marriage. I was teary. Jay was teary. My mom and dad were teary with their joy for us as well. We didn't have long to talk, because a handful of quarters didn't buy you too much time from New York to California, but it was enough.

Jay's family had already known and given their blessings before we had gone out that night. The next day, Jay's mom was glowing, sharing the news with everyone that Jay and Briar are getting married.

And a year later, we did, under the stars on a rooftop in Hollywood, surrounded by love and a supportive community. It was a storybook wedding, with me in my princess white gown with endless layers of tulle, and Jay in his classic tuxedo with onyx cufflinks I'd given him as a wedding gift. We had a ceremony that was influenced by our Jewish roots, but also one we designed to be inclusive. Jay crushed the wine glass to shouts of "mazal tov" and congratulations. The singing and clapping commenced. We were married.

Since then, over the past thirty-two years, we have renewed our vows seven times. It has become a romantic and meaningful ritual for us. With each renewal, our vows have reflected the growth in our relationship, the deep devotion we have for each other, and the playful romance between us. Each renewal refreshes us and has been a profound way to celebrate our love and mark our anniversaries.

There were times during those first years where people would make undermining and pessimistic comments.

Most commonly we'd hear, "Let's see how you're doing in a year…if you still are so mushy and gushy then?"

Where we are concerned, nothing has ever shattered our grip on each other. Our love is our superpower.

V

AND THEN WE WERE FIVE

"In giving birth to our babies, we may find that we give birth to new possibilities within ourselves."
—MYLA AND JON KABAT-ZINN (CURRENT)
AMERICAN AUTHORS AND EXPERTS ON MINDFULNESS, PARENTING, AND CHILDBIRTH

20
GETTING STARTED

J ay and I loved our time alone during that first year and a half of our marriage. After he graduated from NYU, he received an internship for specialized training in the general practice of dentistry. We had a renewed conversation about our plans and what this internship would mean. It meant that Jay would have an extraordinary opportunity to deepen his theoretical and practical expertise in ways that weren't readily available. It also meant that we would spend another year or two in New York. The funny thing was that I was slowly beginning to feel like New York could be my home, and Jay was feeling more and more like all he wanted to do was move to Los Angeles. At that point, we had made many trips back to my home in Santa Monica, and my parents and Jay had gotten very close. On one visit home, my dad introduced Jay to his dentist, and he and Jay connected straight away. Jay found him to be a willing and warm mentor. Jay's goal became clear—he wanted to finish up in New York, migrate to California, and start his career in Brentwood.

We stayed in New York for Jay's internship, and I wound up getting a job closer to our new home in Astoria, Queens. I had heard through the social-work grapevine that a clinical supervisor my sister had learned a lot from and really liked had gotten a grant for a group therapy program for children in foster care. She was looking for two clinicians to become part of her team to help her develop the structure of her program and provide treatment. I went for an interview, and she hired me. The clinic was located in Jamaica, Queens. At that time, the community there was plagued by "crack" addiction. Many unsuspecting people fell victim to the destructive lure of crack cocaine. Every child and sibling group I worked with for the next couple of years had been a casualty of parents who were crack addicts. No one was thrilled that I chose to ride my bike to work in that culture, vulnerable and unprotected, but that was part of how I was able to join and enjoy the community—to be a part of it, up close.

One of my first clients there was a little boy who may have been two or three. He was found wandering in a hallway of one of the projects in Jamaica. He wasn't very verbal in the beginning other than being able to say his name. A lovely foster family was found for him. The foster mother was probably more in the age range of a grandmother, but she was active, warm, and very responsive to this little boy. When he was referred to me, the Department of Social Services hoped that, through play therapy, I might be able to help him reveal what had happened to him. From our first session and through our year together before he and his foster family moved away from Queens, we connected. Whatever had happened to him, it didn't squash his outgoing personality. Through our play, he enacted stories with ambulances and doctors and a mommy doll who often fell down. Sometimes the mommy doll had to get in the ambulance and/or go to the hospital, and sometimes it was him, or even me. That was the only clue I ever got about what his life had been about prior to being found in the projects. He was creative and engaged and seemed to enjoy play therapy and our time together, even when it brought up sadness, fear, or anger. By the time he finished his therapy, he was talking and attending preschool. He was loving and affectionate with his foster mother and family, was making friends, and seemed to be comfortable in his body. It was truly bittersweet when we finished.

What stands out about my work with this boy and in this program is the continuity I see in my desire to want to help people. I often came home eager to tell Jay about the newest client or sibling group. I wanted to adopt them all. However, by the time we did finally leave New York, the only adoptions we had made were of Sigmund, our cat, and the summer after we were married, a beautiful black great dane named Isis.

21
AND IT STARTED WITH SYDNEY REBECCA FLICKER GROSSMAN

I had a minor case of baby fever. I had always loved babies and children, and, in a way, becoming a therapist was an extension of my lifelong dream to become a mother. It was not infrequently that I shared stories with Jay about the wonderful, beautiful, diverse little characters who crossed my path. Soon we were beginning to think about having children of our own, and found ourselves discussing the possibilities.

Toward the end of November, 1988, I started waking up feeling a bit woozy. It wasn't terrible, but it wasn't normal either. By the middle of the day I would feel better, but I was also feeling run down. I was very committed to my kids at work, and our time was so precious and short, I didn't want to miss a single day or session with them. A few days into these symptoms, I realized I had not gotten my period. I restrained myself from being too giddy and hopeful. I'm not a superstitious person, but I think I was able to rally my calm by telling myself not to "jinx" anything by focusing on it. Soon enough, I would know if I had a stomach bug or was pregnant.

The day came, two weeks after my missed period, when I went to the pharmacy on my way home from work. They sold newfangled pregnancy tests where all I had to do was pee on a stick. If a "plus" sign appeared, I was pregnant. If it was a "minus," well, life would continue, status quo. This was the newest, most wonderful technology. Before me, my mom and the women of her day had to wait a few months before providing a urine sample to her doctor, which was then injected into a rabbit. If you were pregnant, the hormones caused particular changes in the rabbit's ovaries, and several days later, you would get your results. Or, of course, you could wait and see if your belly started to grow. In the earliest days of this method, doctors surgically opened the rabbits, killing them to see their ovaries. Today, there must be many grateful rabbits.

I peed on the stick early one Saturday morning, keeping it secret from Jay. I paced, waiting the allotted, torturously long ten minutes to check for a plus or minus. It was bright and clear: +. I knew the tests were fallible, and I would have to go to a doctor, but I felt that this was right. I woke poor sleepy Jay, waving my "pee-stick" in his face, alternating with wet sloppy kisses and tickles. Resisting the new day, he groaned and turned away from me. But I wasn't having it. I was laughing and now jumping on him.

"Wake up, wake up, wake up, Dad! Your lazy days are about to be over."

It took him a minute to pull me into focus and make sense of my raving delirium. "What the hell is going on? Why are you so nuts today? C'mon, let's sleep in."

Not today and not now. More tickling and giggling. We were both silly and laughing, and Jay still didn't realize why. Finally, I had his attention, and he saw what I had been waving in his face. The wordless question was apparent on his face, and I answered wordlessly back, nodding my head yes. We cried and laughed and snuggled in earnest, fully awake.

I found a doctor recommended by Jay's uncle, the cardiologist. She confirmed the result. I was pregnant and due in June. I was out of my head with excitement. It was simply a joyous time for me and Jay. I paid attention almost every waking second.

I was very much in touch with how miraculous pregnancy and birth are. I hated when I first started putting on weight but wasn't quite pregnant enough for pregnancy clothes. I just looked soft and unfit, and none of my clothes could button or zip. But then there was my little tummy-swell. It grew and grew until I felt the first flutter of movement, like the kiss of a butterfly wing. And then I felt the press of a hand or foot extending outward, and I half expected to see an imprint on my stomach—a normal, wonderful version of *Alien*. It was truly wonderful when my pregnancy reached the point where Jay and I could cuddle together and just watch my belly dance from our baby's movement. It was better than any movie or television show.

I continued to work and enjoy being a newlywed. At some point toward the end, we enrolled in a childbirth class, but I realized in the throes of labor how insufficient and inadequate our training had been. As it turned out, all of my babies would be born "sunny side up," or, in medical terms, in occipital posterior position. Women in labor with this presentation most often feel their labor pains in their lower backs. Although my childbirth class briefly discussed "back labor," that was it—just a very brief discussion.

When I went into labor, I was shocked. From my first contraction, I felt a sharp, searing pain in my lower back. I was convinced something was wrong. I allowed a few contractions to come and go, as it was really early in the morning, but the pain was overwhelming. I thought that the beginning was supposed to be easy and then it would get harder as labor progressed. I wondered how much harder it would get, and if I wanted an epidural. I had wanted to have an unmedicated birth, but I was not prepared.

I labored for several hours at home. Jay wanted to apply counter-pressure on my back to ease my pain, but I was so afraid. I thought my back was breaking. It didn't feel like an "ache," as my instructor had discussed, but more like glass searing into me. I told Jay I was too afraid. He tried to coach me, relax me, but it was tough. We decided with my contractions roughly six minutes apart and a minute long, we would go into the hospital. I hated the car rides to the hospital when I was in labor with each of my children. The driving seemed to bring on nausea, which is my least favorite of human maladies. Give me a sore throat any day. I threw up a couple of times on our way in, and vaguely wondered what it was that I had been so excited about when I learned I was pregnant.

We got to the hospital. I got out of the car. I threw up. We got to admitting, and I threw up again. This was *not* how I pictured this. My mother always told me how easy it had been for her to give birth to me, so obviously I thought it would be the same for me. I hadn't been afraid or nervous; I thought birth would be a cakewalk.

Many hours into my labor, my doctor was worried I was getting too tired. When I heard that, I worried she would intervene. I still wanted to be unmedicated. I doubled my efforts and energy, Jay by my side every second. After eighteen hours, I was told I could push, but with each push my doctor was concerned about the baby's heart rate decelerating. She told me that either I get an epidural or she'd take me for a C-section. Not feeling that we had much choice, we agreed to an epidural.

I think the administration of the epidural was equal in pain to that of my contractions. As soon as I had the epidural, the medical team lost the baby's heartbeat. There was a scary moment. They had me change position, and the baby's heart rate was back, but then I couldn't feel anything below my waist, other than the awful sore spot where the epidural had been administered, and I was being asked to push. I pushed for five hours. During the last hour of pushing, my doctor told me repeatedly I could push one last time, but after that we were done with pushing, and it was time for a surgical delivery. Finally, the baby's head was bulging between her inner world and our outer one. I was not going to have surgery at that point. I rallied every ounce of strength and pushed like my life and my baby's life depended on it. I was pissed off by the wishy-washy doctor, and I *goddamn wanted my fucking baby!*

First, her little head emerged, then her shoulders slithered out with the rest of her. It was a girl. It was a girl who was not breathing, but with a little rubbing by the doctor, she did start to breathe. I asked to hold her.

"For a second," the doctor told me, explaining that, with her problematic breathing, she needed to be observed in the neonatal intensive care unit.

She was beautiful. She was perfect. As I held her and she pinked up, I didn't want to let her go. I was instantly smitten. Sydney Rebecca Flicker-Grossman had arrived. But she was quickly whisked away. I asked Jay to go with our baby. He left me reluctantly, and without him or my new daughter, I shook violently and vomited for a good hour from the anesthesia before passing out.

Sydney lived in the NICU for a week. I felt punished by my doctor and the neonatal specialists. I had pumped colostrum, the clear fluid in a mother's breasts when babies are first born, into small vials. It is loaded with immunities and concentrated nutrients that set a child up with the best that nature has to offer. It was full of my love for her. I learned on my second day of visiting the NICU that the nurses had been throwing out my colostrum and offering formula against my wishes. I was devastated and felt powerless. I was also discharged from the hospital before Sydney was able to leave with me. Telling you that it felt like my heart was being ripped out would be an understatement. It may not have been a rational way to feel, but it was real. It aroused images of my dead brother, of my mother leaving a hospital twenty-seven years earlier without her baby. I felt afraid that Sydney might die and I would never take her home.

I commuted to Sydney for only two days, but it felt so much longer. I met a nurse on the first day who had recently come to the hospital from

South Africa. She had been a midwife there, and she took me under her wing. I was soul-wrenchingly grateful to her. She had saved some of my colostrum and had given it to Sydney. There had been concerns on the part of Sydney's NICU doctor that she wasn't strong enough to breastfeed, so I hadn't been allowed to try, but this wonderful nurse told me this was a load of crap, and that the best thing for my girl would be to have her skin to skin with me, suckling at my breast. She tucked us away from the bitchy nurses behind a curtain and taught me to nurse my girl. I felt instantly relieved. I hardly left Sydney's side, except when they kicked me out at the end of visiting hours.

Sydney was born on June 25, 1989, and left the hospital on June 30. My parents had arrived in the city by then to offer us their love and comfort and meet their first grandchild. Her entrance to my world surpassed my hopes and dreams. I learned a lot from her birth, and even more about love and humanity when we finally were able to bring her home. Pregnancy and birth are the beginning, and then you have the rest of life to spend together. My mother and father doted not only on Sydney, but also on me and Jay. They now had an adored granddaughter, and while watching them with her, I deeply felt my own connection with my Mommy and Daddy who would love me forever as their 'baby.' That is what it is to be a parent. It is forever.

22

MY FAMILY GROWS, AND SO DO I: ERIC BENJAMIN FLICKER GROSSMAN, PREGNANCY, AND THE BRADLEY METHOD

When Sydney was six weeks old, Jay and I packed up and flew to California to build our new home. I could say that finally my dreams were coming to fruition, but that wouldn't be completely accurate. What I was learning is that goals are most fulfilling and powerful when they are malleable and can grow with the trends of our lives. I had gone to New York "knowing" that I wanted to return to Los Angeles when I completed my professional training, but meeting Jay presented me with an opportunity to be thoughtful about my life and where I might wind up living. It just so happened that Jay had fallen in love not only with me, but also with my family and the lifestyle he had been exposed to on his numerous visits to California. I hadn't felt deprived or thwarted living an extra three years in New York, but rather I enjoyed that time immensely—and moving back to Santa Monica with my mom and dad for the next year and a half was also an unforgettably special time of learning, love, and growth.

Jay, Sydney, and I were so lucky to reap the benefits of living with the loving, smart people who had raised me. When I thought my breasts would explode when my milk came in and thought maybe something was wrong with me, my mom helped me get through it with her remedies and encouragement, assuring me that having missile-boobs was perfectly normal—despite the pain. And with her help, I learned that that initial pain was fleeting, but the experience of breastfeeding was wonderful. When Jay and I were blind with exhaustion, my parents were there to share the responsibility of caring for Sydney. My mom, in one of her finest moments, told me something I've never forgotten and have shared with many students and patients in turn.

"You know why they make babies so adorable, right?" she asked. I was crying and feeling like I was at the end of my proverbial rope. "Because otherwise you'd kill them."

She made me laugh and brought me a lot of normalizing relief. When I introduced solid food to Sydney and she turned orange, my parents were the ones who made the link between her looking like an Oompa Loompa and her love of sweet potatoes and butternut squash. I had been really worried that something was wrong with her, but it was just a beta carotene overdose—no harm, no foul, and no more orange food.

Being a mommy was the fulfillment of my deepest, oldest desire. Whether it was the joy of quiet time with her, singing, rocking, or sleeping together, I felt indescribable bliss. If Sydney was sick or teething, I couldn't imagine anywhere else I would have rather been than with her, holding her, helping her.

There is physical birth, but there is also psychological birth as babies come to know themselves and others, as they recognize that their hands are part of them or that they can babble at will. I loved it when each child had that moment in their high chair when they realized that if they threw their fork or grape on the floor I would retrieve it. To their delight and glee, it came back to them, like Jay and me when we went out or left the room. It's such a wonderful developmental leap for many children, a first game, as they discover autonomy, object permanence, and the nature of their relationship to the world around them. I loved being a mommy. And I loved being Sydney's mommy.

Meanwhile, during our first year back in Los Angeles, Jay worked hard at preparing to get his California State License to practice dentistry. Although I had a very small private practice, I was mostly home with Sydney. We were now like my parents had once been: cash poor, but rich in love. One evening, over dinner, my dad shared the wonderful adventure Japan had been for him as a doctor in the United States Air Force. He suggested that maybe this would be an exciting option for Jay. He could practice dentistry while working on passing the highly competitive practical part of the California State Dental Licensing Exam. At first, we didn't take it very seriously and were joking about which branch of the military had the most attractive uniforms, but soon Jay and I were truly interested. We were feeling a bit of cabin fever, and as much as we loved living with my parents and they loved having us, we knew it was time to move out on our own.

Jay reached out to the Air Force and the Navy. They had offices across the hall from one another, and whoever would guarantee that he could be stationed in or near Los Angeles with better benefits would be his pick. In the end, he was commissioned as a lieutenant in the United States Navy. My mom and I were thrilled, because we loved those Navy dress whites. As it turned out, Jay did them justice of the highest order. Within the first couple of months after officer training, he was able to sit for the State Dental Licensing Exam in California and passed with flying colors. He learned a lot about life and great dentistry while he was in the Navy, and we were tucking away each paycheck, hoping we would be able to buy our first home sooner rather than later.

Sooner became important. We were pregnant again and would need some space. This time, I was determined to find a better way to give birth. I researched several different classes and trainings and stumbled upon The Bradley Method, also known as Husband-Coached Childbirth. It felt right. It made sense. The basic premise was that birth should be a joyful, loving experience. It is an athletic event, and it requires proper training, including having your significant other as your coach, learning as much as possible about the "event" of giving birth, and tracking nutrition, exercise, and relaxation techniques. This all-encompassing training was what I had been looking for. Having had such a difficult birth with Sydney. I did not know if it would ever be possible for me to give birth with joy, but Jay and I wanted to give it a go.

Dr. Robert Bradley developed The Bradley Method in the early 1960s. He grew up a farm boy in Colorado and had been fascinated from his childhood with birth. While doing his obstetric rotation during his medical training, he was appalled by what he encountered. It was ghoulishly different from the peaceful process he'd seen back home on the farm. He saw women drugged, alone, scared, and screaming. When they were ready to deliver, they were completely anesthetized, knocked unconscious, while their husbands were banished to the no-man's land of the "daddy waiting rooms." Bradley wasn't at all happy about the neonatal nurseries either, where "dopey" babies needed to be monitored by nurses while they recovered from their births, separated from their knocked-out, recovering mommies.

I have spoken to some mothers from that era, and they have all commented that there was a question in the backs of their minds, rational or irrational, as to whether the baby they received after recovering from the anesthesia was actually theirs or not. They described to me feeling vaguely sad and dislocated, having had their babies in their bodies one moment and then, seemingly the next, a nurse was bringing a stranger to them that was introduced as their child.

Dr. Bradley was deeply disturbed by this whole process. He decided to start experimenting, first with teen mothers who were on their own, and then with the medical staff he worked with and their spouses. He used his observations of mammals back on the farm to inform his teaching. Cows, sheep, cats, and dogs all sought out quiet, dark places during labor, where they appeared to be deeply relaxed and asleep until it was time to give birth. When the expulsive contractions began, the mamma sheep or pigs got to the concentrated business of pushing. Only in the presence of abnormality or a medical difficulty would an animal cry out in pain. He wondered if he could teach human mothers these mammalian instincts. Just as we can all swim instinctively at birth but lose the instinct and must be taught again later in life, he thought birth might be something we once knew how to do instinctively but needed help relearning.

What Bradley found in his initial trials was fascinating. The mothers who were trained by him in exercise, pregnancy-specific nutrition, anatomy of pregnancy, anatomy of first, second, and third stages of labor, and deep relaxation, had wonderful experiences of birth—but he noticed one major problem. After one mother gave birth and was immediately given her baby, she looked, doe-eyed, at Dr. Bradly and said, "Oh, Dr. Bradley, I couldn't have done this without you," and thanked him with hugs and kisses.

Dr. Bradley realized that there was a problem that he hadn't anticipated. He didn't want the mothers to thank him. He realized they should be hugging, kissing, and celebrating with their partners. And so this became an important part of his methodology as well.

The more I read and learned about the health advantages and the commitment to joy as an intrinsic part of the birth process, the more certain Jay and I were that we wanted to learn this method. We took a three-month class. Jay was tough and fabulous. He helped me track my required 80–100 grams of daily protein along with adequate greens, calcium, and iron-rich foods. He coached me through my daily pregnancy-specific regimen of exercise. At the end of every day, Jay helped me master deep relaxation using guided imagery, massage, poetry, music, and labor rehearsal.

There was a period of time toward the end of my pregnancy where Jay surprised me with unabashed Post-its. They were everywhere. I'd find them on my mirror in the bathroom, on a milk carton in the refrigerator, or on the TV screen. I would get into my car, and stuck to my steering wheel I would see: "I love you! Have you done your kegels?" Clearly, he wanted to be sure I was getting this exercise in, that strengthens the pelvic floor and can be done anytime, anywhere.

Jay and I practiced, educated ourselves, and trained rigorously. We both wanted to do whatever we could that would help us embrace the birth of our next child and avoid the pitfalls and problems we had encountered with Sydney's birth. One of my big takeaways from birth class was that it is important not to go to the hospital too soon. We learned how to recognize the possible emotional and physical signposts of labor to gauge roughly where we might be in the laboring process. It was really Jay who became a master of the signposts, as my job was to be focused on the actual work of labor. We learned that if I was chatty, and contractions were ten to fifteen minutes apart and lasted only thirty to forty-five seconds, I was probably in early labor. If I became quiet, humorless, and lost my modesty with contractions three to five minutes apart lasting a minute each, we were probably well into labor. If we were going to give birth in a hospital, that would be the time to go.

My problem was that I had felt pretty damn serious about my contractions from the start with Sydney. The lower back pain had been searing, and I wanted to get to the hospital immediately. Then I found out that there's really not much to do or that can be done for a laboring woman in the hospital other than medicate her, and I was very clear that this time I really didn't want meds. Our Bradley instructor taught Jay how to apply deep counter-pressure massage on my lower back. She was firm and adamant that I should allow Jay to try it if I had back-labor again, even if I felt it was counterintuitive.

One night in March, 1991, I started having contractions. It was sunset and a lovely spring night. I was hopeful when I noticed that I was in a great mood, excited and giggly. The contractions felt like a gentle but firm hug around my abdomen. I could deal with that. Jay was excited, and he timed a few. They were short and far apart. It felt good to relax through them. We had learned to change our activity during labor in ways that would either help bring on labor if it was starting, or help it settle down if it was just pre-labor. We went for a walk; we had a bite to eat. We laid down for a little bit and then went in the Jacuzzi for a while. After each contraction, Jay gave me water to drink. Every once in a while, he encouraged me to go to the bathroom. We repeated this routine through the night. As the sun was rising and we were walking around the block, I realized my contractions had stopped. I was a little disappointed, but knew every contraction served a purpose. I went to sleep and waited.

During this period, Jay was close to being discharged from his tour in the Navy, but the first Desert Storm had just broken out. He was called into his commanding officer's office. We had developed a wonderful friendship with his CO and wife, and the conversation they had that day wasn't easy for Jay or the CO. He told Jay that orders hadn't come down yet, but it was likely that all the doctors and dentists would ship out within the week to Hawaii to support the Navy and Marine troops who were shipping out. I was beside myself when Jay told me. He just had to be there for the birth of our baby. I needed him, and the baby would need him. And Sydney would be heartbroken.

"No," I told him naively. "You go back to the captain and tell him that this isn't acceptable and you can't go."

Jay was sweet, and he patiently told me how it just didn't work that way.

Here's a funny thing about Jay. He's a person who just has great luck. I never win drawings and never got away with even taking a cookie from the cookie jar without getting caught. Jay walks into rooms, alarms sound, confetti falls, and he wins prizes he didn't even know he was a contestant for. That said, a few days after the CO told him to prepare to ship out, an offer for a local post came up. With everyone shipping out, they needed a dentist in Seal Beach. Jay got the job and never had to leave. I have great empathy for all the military wives who give birth when their spouses are in harm's way.

A week later, I woke up abruptly at five o'clock in the morning with a familiar tightening in my belly and sharp pain in my back. These were the contractions that I remembered from my first labor. I was a little unnerved but very determined. Jay wanted to massage my back and help me with my back-labor, and this time, I was very open to the idea.

He dug his fists into me. The harder he pushed, the less I felt the contractions. It was surprisingly awesome. I was not giggly or chatty now, though.

I mentally prepared to dig in and surrender to the process as long as possible at home. Jay timed the contractions and told me they were lasting a full minute. Within an hour, they were three minutes apart. We had hired a labor assistant to back Jay up and support us if my labor was tough again. Jay wanted to call her and start moving to the hospital, but I really didn't want to go. I was so sure that we would get there and I'd only be three or four centimeters dilated, not anywhere near the ten centimeters I needed to get to. I started to get ornery and resistant.

"I'm not going to the hospital...Coach me!"

Jay called the birth assistant, also known as a doula, and told her what was going on. She said she would head to the hospital. She recommended that Jay call our doctor and that we should drive carefully, but quickly, and get there, too. She thought I would start pushing soon.

Yeah right, I thought, annoyed.

After some serious coaxing, Jay convinced me to go. The car ride was nasty. My contractions took a lot of work to relax through because Jay was driving and couldn't press on my back. The minute I got out of the car, I felt woozy and threw up.

Aha, a physical signpost. I thought, in the millisecond I was capable of logical thought, that maybe I was truly further along than I believed.

94

Maybe I was in transition at the part where you go from seven to ten centimeters, not usually longer than thirty minutes. It's the hardest part, and at ten you get to push. I thought, *Okay, I can handle this if this is the worst—but if they check me and tell me I'm three centimeters, I will kill Jay, and then I will kill myself.*

We got to triage, where they checked women in labor to determine what they wanted to do with them. I was checked by the doctor, who raised his eyebrows, looked approvingly at me and Jay, and told the nurse to take us to a delivery room. I was ten centimeters and couldn't believe it. I pushed for an hour, then gave birth to our beautiful boy— our second baby, Eric Benjamin Flicker Grossman.

This time, there was no NICU. It still took a lot of work to push him out, but there were no scare tactics or epidurals. Neither of us had any drugs or interventions to recover from, just time to start our lives together the way I had always pictured it. Jay had been an amazing coach and had practically bruised his hands from asserting superhuman pressure on my back. I felt triumphant, grateful, and profound love for this new little baby, my husband, and, of course, for my twenty-two-month-old little girl, who was waiting eagerly to meet her new little brother. Sydney was so affectionate from the start, and very talkative. She didn't start walking independently until she was sixteen months old, but she began talking when she was less than a year old, and one of her favorite topics was babies. She had already become a lover of other babies and small children like her, and couldn't seem to wait for her little brother.

"I want to hold my little baby brother, okay, Mommy?" she asked.

"Yes, honey, it's *very* okay," I croaked out, filled with emotion.

Jay had gone above and beyond to make sure I was comfortable and well cared for at the hospital. He secured a room on the "special guests" floor. That meant the food came from a "special chef" and was presented with real linens and beautiful silverware. I will never forget that dinner: a rack of lamb with mint jelly, mashed potatoes, fresh blanched broccoli, a sourdough roll, and a glass of wine. Eric's birthday was also the first night of Passover, and a big ritual dinner was being held at my parents' house that night. With the exception of the roll, my meal was actually a pretty traditional Passover dinner, too. What made it even better was snuggling Eric in my bed, swaddled in the beautiful soft blanket I had brought for him.

23
GIVING BIRTH
TO A PHILANTHROPY

L iteral children were not our only babies. We also gave birth to a
philanthropy. I would be the coach for this one, and Jay would
carry and deliver.

We had been in a self-development course focusing on self-expression
and leadership, a course we were taking out of sheer interest, and was
not degree driven. During this program, Jay and I became very aware
of a difference in our philosophies about human struggle. I knew that
Jay could get annoyed by beggars on the street in New York and Los
Angeles, but I hadn't thought much of it until we were in this course
together. Jay told me one day between classes as we were coming up
with projects to bring to the world that he was stumped. What he was
most aware of was being "accosted by homeless people, especially
veterans, who were asking for handouts and annoying him."

"Why annoyed?" I asked.

"Because," he said, "I think these people need help, but I don't want to give them money so they can score some drugs or buy alcohol, and I'm not exactly the social worker in the family."

He didn't see how he could really make a difference. He said that on occasion he'd handed out his business cards offering free dental care, but no one had ever come in.

By the time we met at the next class session, Jay had created a project that would become a program called Homeless Not Toothless. He started to create ideas about what was possible and what it might take to get it started. What Jay began to think about as he interviewed people was that many of them wanted jobs and homes—but how would people who had no teeth get hired? Would people hire someone who "looked homeless"? Jay's idea narrowed in on a commitment to raise the pride and dignity of homeless people by restoring their beautiful smiles and dental health.

Within three months, the program was born. It was another light in our lives. Jay would go to his office once a month on a weekend. He enlisted dentists of multiple specialties, assistants, hygienists, and front-office staff to volunteer. Together they would provide a day of free, state-of-the-art dentistry. He worked closely with a local free clinic who screened patients and helped them clean up and get some nourishment before coming in. The main selecting factor for eligibility to the program was being drug and alcohol free for a minimum of six months. There was huge community support as we launched, and over the past twenty years, we have provided over fifteen million dollars' worth of services to sixty-thousand veterans and homeless individuals.

A few years into this program, there came a patient, John, who was missing many teeth from his extensive abuse of methamphetamine. His remaining teeth were so diseased they needed to be pulled. John reclined in the dental chair with his mouth open as he neared the end of his extensive dental work, listening to Jay as he talked about how excited he was to build a little retaining wall at our house. It would be just a little wall to reinforce a hillside in our yard from eroding. He had never done such a thing before, but he had a few bags of cement, and he was raring and ready to go. John couldn't speak with Jay's hands in his mouth, and made some noise. Jay relented and let the man speak. It turned out that John had been a general contractor before he got hooked on drugs and became homeless. He was so grateful for the dental care he had gotten and for the full new set of teeth he was about to receive, that he asked if he could come and build the wall for us as payment.

"And anyways," he said, "you really don't know what you're doing, and two bags of cement ain't gonna cut it, Dr. Jay."

Jay tried to refuse, but John wasn't having it.

You never know who a person is until you really get to know them. John showed up the following weekend, early in the morning, in a car loaded with concrete. He worked for a week on this retaining wall. If one day California crumbles to the sea, that wall is so solid, I'm sure it will still be standing. While he worked at our home, John also noticed structural and aesthetic issues he thought he could help us with. We hired him for more work.

It came to pass that we got a call from a neighbor who was asking about a rickety car parked up the street with some "weird guy" living in it. I was so upset when I realized that John had no place but his ancient car to live in. Jay went out to find him and brought him up to the house. With my hands on my hips, I told him if he wanted to work for us, he could jump in the shower and move whatever stuff he had into our spare bedroom and stay with us until his work was done, or he could choose to not work for us and go away—and I emphasized that I hoped he would move in. He got very teary and accepted our invitation.

John lived with us for two years. I guess we adopted another child. He was an amazing addition to our family. He remodeled our master bedroom, bathroom, and family room. He extended our balcony to run the length of our house. He built us a beautiful pergola. And everywhere were personal, beautiful artistic touches.

In our front garden, there was a good-sized smooth rock. John said that he imagined the rock was a face looking upward to the stars, and felt compelled to carve Galileo's face into it. He thought we'd like it, and we did.

It turned out that through John, we were able to meet a particularly generous, big-hearted, philanthropic movie star, Sharon Stone. John had been very friendly with and worked for her sister years earlier before he got lost in addiction, and had maintained his relationship with her over the years. Sharon was also very committed to ending homelessness. Because of John, she has been a significant source of the wind beneath the wings of Homeless Not Toothless for many years. Although John no longer lives with us but in a home of his own in New Mexico, he calls and visits when he can. And Homeless Not Toothless has become a national model and place for dental interns to train and gain mastery technically and in their commitment to being of service to all people. As with all of our children, we are very proud of this one, too.

24

THE FINAL ADDITION...
WE THOUGHT: ARI MAX
FLICKER GROSSMAN

I had always wanted six children. It seemed like a number that represented oodles of love and abundance. Jay was hard pressed to have more than one, maybe two kids, so we did what couples who love each other do: we compromised and had three. The birth of my third child was as uneventful as my second. By that time, I had become a certified Bradley Method instructor myself. I worked with a lot of couples by the time I got pregnant with Ari, and had become a doula for my couples. I had attended and would attend my sister's childbirths, my best friend's childbirth, and the childbirths of many of my students. I am always filled with joy and awe when a new baby is born. In that moment, couples are forever transformed, and families come into being. It is truly awe-inspiring, and more confirmation of the power of love.

The biggest difference between Ari's and Eric's births was the size of our birth party. This time, we had two friends there to support us. They would rotate massage-duty throughout my labor. I also had my best friend, my parents, Jay's mom, my cousin, and a photographer with me. My children were there, too. The kids were with us for a bit in the beginning, and once we got to the hospital, they went for a walk with their uncle and aunts to get lunch, returning in time to see the birth of their brother.

Just like the cobbler's children are reputed to have holes in their shoes, Bradley instructors don't get guarantees for super easy labors. I was in labor with Ari for five hours and pushed for one. That wouldn't be considered a long labor, but the one part of labor that shouldn't be more than thirty minutes, transition, lasted one and a half hours. About forty-five minutes into transition, the doctor checked me because I was starting to feel like I wanted to push, and I was getting fed up and cranky. He found that I still had another centimeter to go, which meant I could not push yet.

Hell NO, I thought, screaming in my head. I thought frantically about how I could manipulate the situation and get a blessed epidural. I knew if I said I wanted a "fucking epidural," Jay would think it was just one of the emotional signposts of transition. *Shit, shit, shit.* I took a deep breath, and with all the effort I could muster, I opened my eyes with what I hoped conveyed a sweet and compelling attitude.

"Jay, honey, it looks like I'm actually having a tough time getting to ten centimeters, and I'm thinking I could actually be in transition for another hour or two. I really don't think I can do this. Maybe we should start an epidural," I said, calm as I could possibly be, hopefully giving an Academy Award-winning performance.

He had my hands in his, and his face was intimately close to mine. He said that the feeling I was having, that I couldn't do this much longer, was "great" because I probably wouldn't have to. It meant that we were so close to having the baby. Blech. I was getting my own words, which I had been teaching other families for the past several years, thrown back in my face. He said we should take one more contraction, then talk about it again. He wanted me to breathe into the pain, surrender, and picture the baby coming out to join us.

Okay, okay, let's do this. I told him I would go through one more contraction, but if I still wanted the epidural, we were getting it. I felt the familiar tightening and sharp, nauseating, disorienting back pain threaten me.

"Relax, breathe, surrender. You are doing great. Listen to my voice. Feel the love around you. Go deep, picture a cool breeze soothing your body. Picture the sun on a spring day warming your face."

The hum of words, imagery, love, and support felt like they pulled me into a timeless place. All there was was my labor, an image of our baby, and deep, deep surrender. When I opened my eyes again to say I really couldn't do this any longer, an hour had passed. The doctor checked me again, and it was time to get in the game and push to my heart's content. *Yes, please!*

As I mentioned earlier, all my babies were born face up—not the most common position, and not the easiest. For me, pushing was always the hardest and most arduous part of labor, and with Ari, it was no different. I pushed shorter than with Sydney and longer than with Eric. After an hour, my family, Jay, and friends were cheering me on with exclamations that they could see hair. They could see a head coming into clearer view.

"C'mon, you're doing it."

"It's amazing. He's right there."

Between contractions, Jay and my best friend made sure I had ice chips and water. Jay cooed his love and delight.

At some point, Sydney and Eric joined the party and looked on. They intellectually knew what was going on and had even seen a couple of films showing births. Emotionally, they looked curious and concerned, but they seemed to have locked eyes onto the little baby who was working his way out. After an hour and a half, Ari's head came out.

"I want you to listen carefully to my instructions with the next push," my doctor said. "The cord is wrapped a couple of times around the baby's neck, so we are going to take this very slowly. It's going to be fine."

Despite the ominous details, my doctor's calm voice and assurance actually set me at ease and helped me to focus. I wasn't thinking about pain or anything about me. I only wanted to help my baby into the world and hold him. With the next contraction, my doctor told me to let my body work, but that I shouldn't add any extra pressure. As my son's shoulders started to clear, my doctor slipped the cord right over Ari's head.

"Now," he said, "you can give a solid push, but not too hard." I pushed and felt the release as Ari was born.

Between the cord around his neck and being in posterior presentation, he was not breathing, but there wasn't the panic there had been with Sydney. My doctor took Ari to an examining table at the foot of my bed. I won't lie and say I wasn't worried, but before long, he found his first breath and quickly became pink and feisty. He was brought over to me and Jay, and after momentary tension, everyone leaned in to surround us and sing "Shekhekheyanu," the Jewish blessing for having come to a new and miraculous time. Since this was my first birth surrounded by my community, it was also the first time I had experienced singing and blessings, and it was wonderful.

Amid the singing and tears of joy and hugging and kissing, I heard Sydney's sweet eight-year-old voice, "Mommy, can I hold him?" Then Eric, only six and just as sweet, "Me, too?" Sydney's immediate desire to hold her second brother came as no surprise. At that point, she slept in a bed covered by Beanie Babies that she had collected and saved from the time she was a toddler. She considered her Beanie Babies to be her beloved babies, which reflected her growing affinity for mothering. Bedtime with Sydney was a challenge for several years because every Beanie Baby needed to be carefully moved nightly to their floor-bed so she had room for herself in her bed. Then each one needed to be kissed, properly covered, and told a bedtime story.

Meanwhile, Eric had been developing his parental tenderness, too. He was always a slight and slender child who seemed to intuitively empathize with others who were also on the small and vulnerable side. When he was only two, we still had our big great dane, Isis. It was clear, despite the dog being so much bigger than him, Eric was always soothing, petting, and playing with her as though she was his little baby. It wasn't out of the ordinary to find he had taken a nap, curled up with her, his head on her belly, and arms stretched out blanketing her. He was very protective of that big old black dog, and every dog, cat, and chicken that was to come. And when Ari was born, it was no surprise to hear his voice in harmony with his big sister's.

It is moments like these that allow us to metabolize and put in perspective life's adversities and tough times. For that moment and that time, love and health reigned supreme, and life was perfect. And then we were five.

VI

DARK TIMES...BIG BUMPS...
LOVE DON'T FAIL ME NOW

"And one has to understand that braveness is not the absence of fear but rather the strength to keep on going forward despite the fear."
—PAULO COELHO (1947-)
BRAZILIAN AUTHOR AND LYRICIST

25
LET THE TRIALS BEGIN—LOSS

It wasn't all smooth sailing from one wonderful moment to the next. Between the births of Eric and Ari, I had three miscarriages. When Eric was a year and a half old, in 1993, Jay and I got the "baby bug" again. We felt it would be a great time to eliminate birth control and see about creating one more little human being to bring into our family. It didn't take long, and we were so happy, but at eight weeks, I started to bleed spontaneously just before going in to see my doctor. I miscarried.

When my doctor confirmed it, we were heartbroken. He told us to take it easy for a month or two, and that these things happen for a reason. He said that usually there is some sort of genetic or congenital anomaly that is so severe nature rejects the pregnancy. These are pregnancies that aren't viable from the start. He said we were "probably better off." I heard and understood what he said, but my heart only knew that I had lost a baby who I already loved, and had hopes and dreams for. An eight-week human embryo is not very different from a chicken or cow embryo. It has no thoughts or feelings yet, having only a brainstem, but the feelings that surfaced were not rooted in anything logical and were only made worse by platitudes. I cried and grieved and took some time to blame myself. I scavenged through my recent memory to scrutinize my behavior and diet. The self-blaming didn't help. Only tears, love, and talking it through with Jay, family, and friends helped me get through it.

Six months later, we were ready to try again, and we got pregnant immediately. Eight weeks into the pregnancy, I saw my doctor, and everything looked great. Everything seemed to be off to a healthy start. My belly started to swell at around twelve weeks, and that was reassuring. My next doctor's appointment was scheduled at fourteen weeks. He examined my belly and took measurements, nodding and smiling, which made me feel reassured again. But then he did the ultrasound. Nothing. I couldn't see the baby. I didn't see a heartbeat. What was happening? What was wrong with the technology? It turned out that it wasn't a technological glitch—the baby had stopped developing soon after my eight-week visit, but my uterus had continued to grow and develop as if a baby was there. It was a very rare syndrome, but again, this was not a "viable" pregnancy. I was alone and stunned. I hadn't expected there to be a problem. I could either wait until my body recognized that there was no live baby and went into spontaneous miscarriage, or my OB could perform a D and C (dilation and curettage). I couldn't bring myself to go home and wait out the symptoms that would have me birth a dead embryo.

My doctor gave me a Valium and said the D and C wouldn't hurt much. He lied. It did hurt, and I surrendered and cried through the whole procedure. How could this be happening again?

As I recovered and struggled through this loss, I knew for sure I wasn't going back to this doctor who minimized my pain and loss as being "for the best," and as I came to find out later, hurt me unnecessarily. He could have given me IV anesthesia, but didn't.

My best friend received her gynecological care from a nurse midwife, and she thought I might benefit from her warmth and expertise. I met her, liked her a lot, and went to her for a little over a year. When I realized it was taking a while to get pregnant this time, she recommended that

I consider seeing her backup doctor and get evaluated by him. I really liked his manner, experience, and knowledge. I felt understood.

Again, I got pregnant, soon after finding my new OB. This time, we lost the baby at fourteen weeks, and I was devastated. I remember our doctor telling Jay and me that there was no heartbeat. There also wasn't a heartbeat between hearing this news and my downpour of tears. The doc told us that he could get us in later that day for the surgical procedure of aborting the pregnancy. It was an unreal moment. My parents couldn't understand why we didn't just stop and enjoy the two healthy, happy children we had. But at this point, Jay and I were all in. This had been my dream—our dream. I felt like this one more baby was so important. I also felt more and more defeated—severely battle-worn.

Everything about the pain of loss and grief shown in the media is completely true, and it's anything but melodrama. I really thought my heart would stop beating and the tears wouldn't stop falling. I remember wondering how it could possibly be so alive, beautiful, and cheery out. I saw people walking on the street carrying on like it was a normal day. I noticed people smiling. There were so many colors everywhere. I felt like the world should have turned gray and somber and dead.

How did my own mother survive having carried Israel to term, only to deliver him and lose him? How did she ever put one foot in front of the other ever again? Somewhere inside, I knew that my mom's capacity to grieve and grow and still bring two more babies into the world would eventually inspire me and help me through, but for that moment I felt insane with the burden of this loss. I was shaken to my core.

When my new doctor performed the surgery, he didn't just give me a little Valium. I had told him about my last experience, and he was very sympathetic. He was sorry and explained I wouldn't feel anything that day. I was given an IV and knocked out. And when I woke up, it was over.

Some time later, a few days maybe, my doctor called to check in on me. He understood and empathized with my despair. He also said that this didn't mean we couldn't have a baby. He wanted me to see a fertility specialist. He said that once I was pregnant and the pregnancy took, he would take me back into his care. I did go to the specialist and eventually got pregnant with Ari, resulting in a six-year age difference between Eric and Ari.

Through all the miscarriages, I was raising my children, loving them, loving Jay, loving our life. The love carried me through each day. Hearing Sydney or Eric laugh, laughing with them as a family, and being together are the things that helped me heal. We had moved into a lovely home in a lovely little community. Sydney started nursery school, and then so did Eric. There were days at the park watching Sydney and Eric bond over the jungle gym, or where they would coax me to go up and down the slides with them, which they found hilarious. There were lazy days at home where after school they would each want me to read a book to them and act out all the parts or where we might bake chocolate chip cookies from scratch. There were sick days, too, with runny noses, earaches, or diarrhea. But through it all, they were inspiring and adorable, and adore them I did. I was able to love, laugh, and be. Love was the superpower that got me through. It was the foundation on which I was able to lay my thoughts and all other feelings.

26
THE UPS AND DOWNS
OF BUSINESS

W hile we were growing our family, Jay bought his practice in Brentwood in 1991. During those early years, in addition to raising the children, seeing a few private patients, and putting in some hours at a child development clinic without walls, I was also very involved with helping Jay grow and develop his practice. He had inherited an office manager, assistant, and hygienist from the previous doctor. All we needed to do was to shake, stir, and bake, we thought.

There were a lot of starts and stops in those early years. There were many patients who didn't want to be transferred, sight unseen, to a new doctor. Complicating matters, the previous doctor had been a gay woman who had cultivated her "brand" as one that was part of and supported by the LGBTQ community. Although Jay supported the community, he wasn't gay himself, and many patients chose to leave. I shamelessly marketed for Jay, placing business cards and flyers on every windshield of every car I ever passed. I handed out cards everywhere and to everyone. I learned the dental business and how to work the front office, receiving tutorials from the office manager.

As the practice grew over time, we felt our passionate dedication was paying off. For the first time in a long time we were ahead of our bills and able to add a few extravagances to our lives. On Valentine's Day before Ari was born in 1996, Jay told me he had a special gift and blindfolded me, tucked me into our car, and drove off. When we finally stopped and he took the blindfold off, he said:

"I love you with all my heart. Happy Valentine's Day. How do you like it?"

It took a minute to orient myself and focus my eyes in the bright light. There was a beautiful Mediterranean-style home in front of me. The sign in front said, "sold."

"You got me a house for Valentine's Day?" I asked, stunned.

He had. It was a few months before we were able to move in, because there were more choices to make before it could be finished: tile, flooring, landscaping, and designing a pool and Jacuzzi. I had my own walk-in closet. Our bathroom was huge. I had a butler's pantry, a formal dining room, and an eat-in kitchen. Each of my children had their own bedroom, plus I also had a guest room/office. I had floor-to-ceiling windows. I was deliriously happy. Not only was it more than big enough, we were able to participate in the design and add our own personal touches.

I could have lived in that house until the end of our lives. Everyone who moved into the neighborhood had children or was having children. It was a friendly and open community. We celebrated births and birthday parties, and we came together in support of each other when we encountered challenges. Life was moving along at a steady clip.

Toward the end of 2001, I noticed that something was not right in our finances. Jay kept saying that I shouldn't worry and that we had a lot of collections to make, meaning there were still a lot of outstanding bills that patients hadn't yet paid. It would be any day that the money came in, and I would be able to do the shopping for the kids I had been putting off because we had no disposable income. I waited a few months.

I hadn't worked in the dental office for a couple of years at that point, and enjoyed being home as a full-time mom. A few months each year, I taught Bradley classes, but it was all easy and low-key. I loved what I did and how we were living, and nothing felt like work to me. It had all been creative energy up until that moment. But now my business senses were on full alert. I told Jay that something didn't feel right to me. How could there be "hundreds of thousands of dollars" outstanding when we had always operated at close to 100 percent collections? We rarely had outstanding payments due. Jay, who was usually obsessed with the numbers, seemed to have no idea about what was going on. I was becoming alarmed, and I told Jay I was coming back into the office to get to the bottom of this.

On my first day back, all dressed up for business and ready to go, our friend the office manager, was not happy to see me. She abruptly told me that a busy day was ahead of us and that she wouldn't have time to help me get acclimated to the "new systems" that were in place. But, she said, I should feel free to make myself at home and get myself caught up however I needed. It may have been an overreaction, but I felt fury roar inside of me. I had to work hard to calm my inner Catwoman, who wanted to scratch her eyes out.

We didn't tell the office manager the "real" reason I was back in the practice. We told her I needed more grown-up time for myself and wanted to work a little more, so coming back to the office made sense. The manager thought she was going to get me on the phones to follow up with patients on their treatment plans and confirm appointments. She wasn't at all happy when I asked her for the password to the dental program and started pulling charts alphabetically. I let her know I was not there to work for *her*, but that she was working for me. She was indignant, but I didn't give a shit. If I had been slightly suspicious before I came into the office, once I had taken a cursory glance around, my "bullshit-o-meter" registered a stink into the stratosphere.

I took a couple of deep breaths and dug in to get to the source of what stank.

In the time I had been out of the office, computers had been added as a mainstay to running the practice. There were still paper charts, but Jay wanted everything duplicated completely to electronic records, and this was in process. I had no idea how to log in, how to pull up the e-charts, or how to rifle through everything to figure out what was going on with the finances.

It took weeks to figure out the ins and outs of how the office now ran. There was no one designated person accountable for oversight. Our office manager was the only one handling all treatment plans, payment agreements, negotiation with insurance companies, and balancing of the books. I started to find conflicting information between paper and electronic charts.

I then started to pull the thread that unravelled terrible fraud. In the beginning, when I told Jay what I was finding, he minimized my observations and assured me that some anomalies might show up. He was sure I was misreading something and it would all work out. To be fair, Jay is often right about these things. He was the numbers guy, the businessman with a real intuitive flare, and I was the touchy-feely artsy gal. But the truth is, I'm smart. Math and accounting might not be intuitive for me, but I'm a great detective. I was not going to be dismissed.

Finally, I came across a few paper charts that showed bizarre notes. In one chart, every tooth in a young patient's mouth had been worked on, according to the billing, but the clinical notes entered by my husband didn't corroborate this. I felt my heart thumping fast, frightened and angry. I found more and more charts like that one. Eventually I suspected that our manager was also keeping a separate set of records. I wanted to go to her home and take a look at the office computer we trusted her to have there. Did she steal our program, along with a lot of money from us and our patients? I had unearthed a significant amount of evidence that pointed at our office manager's dishonesty, but

I wanted this one more piece. When I showed Jay everything I found, he was now completely on board.

Jay and I agreed that we should make a date to do a training at the manager's home with her. While there, our intention was to copy our office files and delete the dental program from her computer. I felt disgusted. I had been good friends with this woman in the early days when we first bought the practice. Even though we saw each other less over time, especially when I decided to stay home with the kids, she and I went to lunch together, spoke on the phone, and had double dates with our husbands—and she had been stealing from us mercilessly the whole time. Jay and I decided that the office manager and I could go to the kitchen and prepare lunch, while he cued up the supposed training. We figured that would give Jay thirty to forty minutes to retrieve our dental program, which was plenty of time. Our manager didn't suspect anything. Despite the fact that she had been very cold and unhelpful to me recently in the office, on this day she seemed warm, like my old friend. That made it even more painful.

After the uneventful "training," Jay and I went back to his office to go through all my notes, the charts, and the new material we had taken off of our manager's home office computer. What we found was eye-poppingly scary. Over the years, the office manager had stolen over a million dollars. As the reality of it sank in, not only did I feel betrayed and victimized, but also found it hard to believe that on some level Jay didn't know. Our manager billed patients for non-existent dental work. She diverted cash payments to her personal accounts. There was enough money coming in monthly that the manager was able to funnel sufficient amounts to Jay to keep him satisfied, distracted from considering any wrongdoing while she kept a mountain of money for herself. He knew he worked hard; he checked the daily financial reports, such that they were, and it seemed to "feel" right to him—but how could he not look more deeply? I thought my head would explode.

We figured everything out on a Friday and took the weekend to sort through it all. We brought in a consultant a few weeks earlier because

I wanted specialized eyes on the matter. On Monday, our office manager/old friend would be escorted out of the office, passwords and locks changed, and interviews and team building taken on with the remaining staff. We decided we wouldn't press charges against the office manager as we came to understand the complexities and costs involved if we litigated. Her being gone would have to be good enough. I would keep coming in for a while until we regrouped, and I would also contact patients to make apologies and right our wrongs. It was a painful but cleansing ritual.

The hardest part was confronting the potential rift between Jay and me. Even though my miscarriages were heartbreaking, they pulled Jay and me *together* in our love for each other. This felt so different. I couldn't bear the possibility that Jay had colluded, even if it was unconscious and by omission. We had many emotional and deep conversations. It was one of the only times in our marriage that he was absolutely defensive and unmoveable. He seemed unable to accept or even consider that he was ultimately responsible for everything in his office. It was his responsibility to know what practices were taking place in his name, and his difficulty with understanding this deeply frightened me. I felt that the stability and integrity of our marriage was under threat. For these reasons, I finally realized that either he needed to get therapy or I was leaving. I needed to know that he was open and committed to understanding himself, me, and the value of integrity in our life. Integrity, to me, is an empowering and profound context for living a powerful life. On a foundation of love, integrity allows life to be lived fully, with openness and freedom—unencumbered by lies, incompletions, or mischief.

Jay was devastated by all of it and finally agreed, reluctantly, to go to therapy. It was hard for him to claim responsibility for the shambles his office was in and the pain and mess he had caused. He had become so focused on his office, he would leave early in the morning and often not be home until the kids were in bed. I felt like he had lost touch with his priority to have ample time to spend with me and the kids, and yet was also not conscious, despite his long hours, of what was happening under his watch in his office. I wouldn't stay with him if he betrayed himself and all that he said he was committed to in life. He ultimately chose to work hard on himself, his office, and his relationships with me and the kids.

I had been so frustrated, furious, and wounded when I discovered the embezzling and deceit perpetrated by our office manager. But that's also how I felt when I discovered how resistant and fearful Jay was of getting to the "truth." It was such an uphill battle for me to prove what I had suspected, and Jay wasn't supportive initially of my coming in to investigate. I wanted him to welcome my input, and my feelings were hurt terribly.

When Jay did recognize that therapy would be helpful and agreed to go, I was relieved, but also challenged. I realized that I was partly reluctant to let go of my hurt, and I wanted to be angry. I had to be honest with Jay and work out the reason why I wanted to keep punishing him, and we did so through many conversations, and a few self-development courses in communication that we took together. There was a lot of disappointment and hurt to work through, and when Jay was able to hear me, and I was able to feel compassion for him, I was able to really let it go. It was a time of pain, a time of growth, and a time of recommitment. Love remained our superpower.

27
THE S#%T KEPT HITTING THE FAN

S ydney was turning thirteen and her Bat Mitzvah was that June. She led the entire service that day at Synagogue and was so insightful, emotionally committed, and connected to social justice in her d'rash—or teaching. She left a big impact. She inspired hope and preached inclusion, challenging accepted social mores. She was affected and influenced intuitively by what was going on in the world at large so soon after 9/11. I remember sitting with her at our dining room table as she grappled with the message she wanted to convey.

"Mom, the topic for my service is so hard," she said to me.

"How so, honey?"

"Well," she started tentatively, "I think Rahab is a hero, but she's also a prostitute. She winds up saving the two spies that Joshua sends into the walls of Jericho who would have been killed if she hadn't hidden them. Not only that, she tells the spies that she *knows* God will give Joshua the land for Israel. She's like a prophet, Mom. I mean, she seems like she was a really strong woman, and maybe she also had to make money for her family and didn't have much choice about her job back then. I feel like we shouldn't judge people so quickly, not her and not anyone. I feel like there's a lot of judging going on in the world right now, and it just isn't right. Can I say that to the congregation?"

"What do you think?" I asked, and that surprised her.

She was expecting a "yes" or "no" from me. Ultimately, she decided to present her controversial idea that the hero in this story may have worked as a prostitute, but who she was was a hero. She came to the conclusion that it required courage and belief in her own moral compass, similar to Rahab, even if it wasn't popular to share her ideas. Sydney's message was that we need to stand up for what's right even if it isn't popular. I hugged her and told her how proud I was of her.

Seeing her come of age in her Judaism that year was a wonderful and profound moment. The boys were also bringing us great joy. Eric excelled as a fifth-grader getting ready for middle school, and Ari was an adorable, inquisitive little comedian in nursery school.

Eric always kept us on the move. He walked when he was only nine months old, and I'm convinced that this was because he was driven by his curiosity and drive to explore the world. By the time he was ten, that early drive blossomed, and his passions were divided between basketball, art, and academic success. He could make beautiful poems out of the unrelated weekly spelling words. He'd show me his math homework and explain it to me better than I could explain it to him. This small-framed, fast, skinny little boy could nail a free throw with alarming ease, especially considering the basketball was almost as big as he was. And then there were the artwork and intricate LEGO projects he could spend hours crafting.

One Hanukkah, Eric opened a several-thousand-piece LEGO set and disappeared. Without help, Eric built his LEGO train by himself, and asked, "Why don't they make them harder?"

And then, "Watch this."

Eric took out a remote control, hit a button, and off the sleek train went, around a complex multilevel track he'd built. This kid amazed me. These had to be Jay's genes, because I can't build a tower out of plain old blocks.

Then there was Ari, funny, affectionate, and always entertaining. One day, we were at a Bar Mitzvah luncheon and there was a beautiful, elegant dessert table. He was three years old and in a little tuxedo, all dressed up for the occasion. While I was talking with a friend, I noticed she looked distracted, then amused. She started to laugh and told me to turn around. At the dessert table, every few seconds, a hand would come out from under the linen-covered table, grab a treat, and disappear again. Then the hand returned the treat, a single bite taken out of it.

Oh my God, I thought. *That's Ari, tasting every treat and putting it back.*

I ran to the table and lifted the tablecloth. There he was, with a couple of his friends. He was entertaining them and providing dessert "tastes." I felt I should be angry with him, but could only laugh. Ari already had a knack for taking the mundane and turning it into a comedic act.

Unfortunately, though our children brought us joy, Jay and I just couldn't seem to get ahead of the huge financial impact of our office manager's massive theft.

In July 2002, we realized that with all the restitution we were making and the losses we'd been hit with as a result of the previous embezzling, we weren't going to be able to stay in our Valentine's Day house or keep our children in the private schools they had been attending. In fact, we were so deeply in the hole of debt, after many conversations between us and our financial advisors, we realized we needed to declare bankruptcy. We had to recognize our limitations and how eroded our financial foundation had become. It's easy for a house of cards to crumble. Every aspect of our lives was impacted, but we were not going to be stopped, and we were committed to rebuilding. There are big costs financially, emotionally, and socially to declaring bankruptcy, but it can also be a road of return to worth and self-esteem. We braced ourselves and declared.

With a commitment and drive to powerfully restructure our life and begin again with integrity, we started with our goals for our children. We found a neighborhood in a blue-ribbon school district roughly an hour away from where we had been living. I was most heartbroken to lose the home Jay, the kids, and I had built together and thought we would live in forever. My heart was sad that my children had to leave the schools and neighborhood in which they had established wonderful friends from infancy—something I never wanted them to experience, knowing how hard it had been for me having moved to four different schools by the time I started junior high. When we moved from our first home to the Valentine's Day house, we only moved a few blocks, so there had been no major transitions to face other than packing and unpacking. Our time of initial growth and abundance all came crashing down.

We moved to a smaller, older house in another friendly neighborhood. My older kids attended the local public schools, and Ari joined a pre-K at a Jewish day school. As we adjusted to life in the Conejo Valley, I was highly stressed. I had given up my housekeeper as part of our financial repair, and without household help, a new level of organization was required of me as Jay continued to commute to his office and I started a very part-time private psychotherapy practice to contribute financially. All of this while juggling my family responsibilities. I was torn between wanting to be completely available to my children as they adjusted to new schools and new friends, and wanting to be helpful to Jay in the dental practice as he rebuilt the culture there with his team. And I was missing my old close friends and community. Jay and I spoke, cried, and held each other every day, voicing our worries and concerns. We recognized the limitations of reality as we worked to build our new dreams, new goals, and new steps to fulfill them. It was a difficult time, but we were beginning to heal.

In November, as we began to find our way out of the disaster zone, I found a tiny hard lump in my breast. It was very small and felt like it could have been a lymph node that was swollen, but I was concerned. I had Jay feel for the lump, and we decided to watch it for a week or two. If it went away, great, but if it was still there, we would go see my doctor. Two weeks later, in the beginning of December, it was still there. I called my doctor and made an appointment, hopeful that we'd be in and out. We decided we would make a date of the day, go in on Jay's Harley, the bike he had managed to keep, then take a ride up the coast and go out for lunch. Some things are worth missing work for, even when you need the cash flow. Surely I'd be fine.

At first, my doctor didn't feel the lump. I placed his hands. "There," I said. "It's tiny, but it's there."

He agreed and did an ultrasound right then.

"Hmm," he mumbled, "this looks a little suspicious. If you have a few more minutes, we can do a biopsy right here and now, and by Monday we will know for sure what's going on."

We had the biopsy. We didn't take that Harley ride up the coast that day. I was too scared and in shock, and I just wanted to go home.

It was going to be a long weekend. This is a story I have heard from every woman I've supported and spoken to about their process with breast cancer. Not knowing what's going on while waiting to receive lab results is the most worrisome part of the diagnostic process. I felt helpless, and all I could do was wait.

There I was, at the start of the winter holidays with family coming over, paralyzed with the fear of what it would mean if I had cancer. I was committed to not only cooking my usual weekly Sabbath meal, but also infusing the night with an air of celebration in honor of the first night of Hanukkah. Despite not being a believer in God, I found myself praying anyway for the miracle of health. My hands felt heavy as I prepared latkes and homemade applesauce. I went through the motions of cooking, setting the table with Hanukkiot and linens, tuning my guitar, and wrapping gifts for everyone. I was on automatic pilot—I was there, but not there.

I cried with Jay before my guests arrived and then spent some time alone with my mom and dad, once they showed up. They helped me identify that my fears were the anticipatory conjurings of my imagination. Nothing bad had happened yet. Until I received the results of my biopsy, my life was to be lived unchanged and focused on the present. Of course, this was easier said than done, but it offered an anchor to reality and some peace of mind for me. With the love and support of my family, I was able to enjoy the holiday meal and celebration that night.

Slowly the weekend passed. On Monday, Jay came home early. Sydney and Eric were doing homework, and Ari had a friend over for a playdate. It was a regular school day. Jay took me to our room for some privacy. He sat me on our bed. He took my hands, and I knew it wasn't good.

He said, "I got a call from the doc. You have malignant carcinoma, probably ductile. We need to get you in as soon as possible for a lumpectomy and a more detailed pathology report."

Then, a deafening silence. I felt all my blood rush out of my body, down to my feet, out my soles, and down through the earth's crust to the core. I felt my 'self' leave. For an instant, I felt suspended. I was staring at my mortality, and was petrified. I felt like the center of my being wouldn't hold. I cried, and Jay cried. There was nothing else we could do. We made my appointment for the lumpectomy and decided that until we really understood what was happening we wouldn't tell the children. Jay pledged his love and support—whatever I went through, we would go through together. We cried again and made love.

I woke up the next morning scared, but also feeling fury and determination rise in me. I would not be beaten. I suppose on an intuitive level, I felt that my cancer was an awakening to the fact that human beings are always psychosomatic. We have a mind-body connection from birth, and where one is impacted, so is the other. For life to prosper and flourish, so must body (soma) with mind (psyche) together in a strong, conscious marriage.

Jay and I interviewed oncologists. We read. We asked questions. I talked to parents at Ari's school who had dealt with cancer, two of whom were still in the midst of their fight. I was deeply moved and strengthened that these moms, dads, and families who were fighting their own battles were stepping forward to support me. I am grief-stricken that today I am the only one of this wonderful group of parents who is still alive. I will always be grateful for the love and support they offered me.

Despite not being a religious person, I am a spiritual one, and for the second time in a week, prayer, blessings, and gratitude soothed and helped ground me. I don't follow the letter of Jewish Law, but I do feel moved to nurture my spirit and emotional state with meditation, song, personal internal conversation, and even readings. In that moment, I felt the need to put goodness, healing, and loving intention into the world and community around me. I also wanted to allow the love and healing prayers of others into me. I needed to feel prayer and love resonate in me when I felt so full of dread and hollowness. When the day came for my lumpectomy, I brought blessings I had composed with me to the hospital.

The drive to the hospital through Malibu Canyon at sunrise was consoling, and oddly enough, a beautiful experience that I will never forget. Pink, lavender, and gold against a newly born blue sky contrasted by the vast deep blue-black deceptive calm of the Pacific Ocean. The sun seemed softened by coastal mist rising off the sea. Lines and colors blurred like a beautiful watercolor painting. I was wrapped in beauty, the aroma of sea salt, and the peace of the morning. In that moment, despite my worries, I felt profound thanks for my life.

When we got to the hospital, I was in better spirits than I thought I would be. My parents were already there waiting for us. We discussed our worries and hopes. Jay's phone kept buzzing with calls from friends and family reaching out to send their love and wishes for health and a speedy recovery.

Among these calls were messages from our old rabbi, who had moved to the east coast. I was told that our new rabbi had also reached out and sent her blessings. Finally, a Chasidic rabbi friend of ours arrived in my little waiting room to offer his prayers and support in person, while also telling me of his rabbi friends who were at the Western Wall that day praying for me. Even for someone who isn't religious, this was overwhelmingly wonderful. If I believed in signs, I would say this outpouring from religious leadership was exactly that.

When my medical team came to take me into surgery, I offered blessings and thanks to them, and, with tears staining my cheeks, hugged my family and said goodbye. I remember being wheeled away, but when I woke up, I felt like there had been no passage of time. I knew I was groggy, but if it hadn't been for that telltale sign I would have wondered when the surgery was starting.

While I was in recovery, my doctor came to me with a warm smile. She told me I had continued blessing the medical team throughout the surgery to their delight, and all had gone well. It would be a few days before we got all the results, but she felt that it looked good and that she was able to get clear margins—meaning she didn't leave any of the tumor behind. They also removed a couple of lymph nodes from my armpit to find out if cancer cells had infiltrated my lymph system, and they, too, looked good. It was the first time since finding this lump that I felt reality informed my hope.

While I was in the hospital, I was given some literature from the American Cancer Society. One of the items was a questionnaire. It asked questions to help people determine whether or not they want to be tested for a genetic mutation known as BRCA (pronounced: brah-kuh), a mutation that results in a heightened likelihood of developing breast or ovarian cancer. If you answered "yes" to at least three questions, they recommended testing. Currently, the Mayo Clinic has a thorough list of criteria for who should consider being tested for the BRCA mutation.

The questions were, paraphrasing:

1. *Are you under the age of fifty?*

2. *Do you have any first- or second-degree relatives (parents, siblings, grandparents) who have had breast or ovarian cancer?*

3. *Have any men in your family had breast cancer?*

4. *Are you of Ashkenazi (Eastern European) Jewish descent?*

Maybe there were one or two more questions, but numbers 1, 2, and 4 applied to me. I brought this up to my oncologist, but he didn't think I needed to pursue genetic testing, as he felt my risk was low. As if consoling a child, he said that if it would make me feel better, I could of course get tested. Ultimately, it seemed to me that without all the information I couldn't make an educated choice about how I would want my treatment to proceed. Thankfully, I went against his recommendation.

I reached out to my gynecologist and gave him my oncological update. The good news was that the tumor was only slightly more than one centimeter, and although it was technically an invasive tumor, there was no evidence of spread, which was also good news. However, I was HER2NEU-Negative, which meant I had less treatment options post-chemotherapy for prevention, and the cancer was a very fast-growing type that had been developing for six months or less. My oncologist was recommending an aggressive concentrated chemotherapy over a four-month period to be followed with radiation. If I tested for the BRCA mutation and found that I was affected by it, I would seriously consider having a double mastectomy, which would negate the need for radiation. The BRCA mutation, once it is expressed as cancer, is highly likely to express itself again, and I wasn't going to go through this again if I could help it.

My gynecologist was on board with my starting chemo as soon as possible, and agreed that doing the BRCA test would give us important definitive answers. It was a simple blood test he had to send away for. At that time, there was only one lab in the country offering the test, so we had to wait a few more days. It was now mid-December, and everything was moving fast in spite of not feeling fast enough. From diagnosis to this visit, only two weeks had passed.

Before starting chemo, my oncologist explained that although the treatment would be strong and the best course for killing any cancer that might be left in my body, I shouldn't have many side effects—besides losing my hair, which I could expect within the first month of treatment. Other than that, and maybe being a little tired and nauseous, I should be okay for work and sticking to my normal routine. Not true for me.

Chemo was sickening. I was given a "cocktail" of two very noxious, powerful drugs: Adriamycin and Cytoxan. I remember seeing the bag of glowing red medication for the first time, knowing it would be pumped intravenously through my body. I felt woozy looking at it. I couldn't help but think about how nothing in nature is that color, and it frightened me. This was serious medicine. Even worse, with each dose I got progressively sicker from the side effects. By the time I had my fifth and last dose, I had to be hospitalized because the doctors were concerned, as was I, regarding the extreme dizziness, general disorientation, nausea, and vomiting I was experiencing.

On New Year's Eve that year, I had completed the first of my chemo sessions, and Jay and I had made plans for a quiet romantic dinner just for the two of us. I was feeling a little better, having survived my first treatment and knowing I was actively working to heal myself. Jay, on the other hand, looked awful and seemed distant to me—quiet and restrained. He took my hands and told me that the results of the BRCA test had come back that afternoon and were positive.

Any appetite I'd had dissipated. I had tested positive for a mutation called BRCA1, that I presumed I'd inherited through my maternal grandmother, who had died at a young age of ovarian cancer. Since I had breast cancer already, my chance in the future of new occurrences was approximately 90 percent. My chance of having ovarian cancer in the future was also very high. It had been explained to me that if I had a double mastectomy, removing all my breast tissue including my nipples, I would reduce my risk of breast cancer to 3–5 percent and ovarian cancer to 50 percent. Option number two was to have a double mastectomy and *also* have my ovaries and fallopian tubes removed, which would reduce my risk of both cancers to almost nothing. The third and final option was that I could let it be, get followed closely with screenings, and move forward with radiation, which would help with the resolution of my current cancer but not of future cancers.

I felt my choice was easy. I chose being alive for myself and my family. The risks were all too high if I didn't take a very proactive approach.

I asked Jay, "Will you still love me even without my own breasts?"

I think this was largely my own infantile terror at having surgery and fearing that *I* would hate my body and myself, and I was projecting this onto Jay. If I had this fear of being repulsed by my mutilated body, it didn't feel so farfetched to think Jay might feel that way and not love me either.

He burst into tears and said, "I love you no matter what. I want you alive."

28
SURVIVING AND THRIVING

When I began receiving treatment, Jay mobilized all of our friends in the healing community. After each chemo session, some combination of healers would come to our home and provide support and body work. All of them were in favor of my receiving western medicine as my first line of treatment, but explained that shiatsu, acupuncture, body manipulation, chiropractic, prayer, homeopathy, Reiki, and other alternative medicines were powerful adjuncts. They could make a huge impact on my physical acceptance of the chemo, and my state of mind and attitude about having cancer.

My acupuncturist came into my bedroom one evening after I had received chemo. He asked how I was doing, and I started to cry. I hated my Goddamn cancer and I couldn't wait to decimate it. He understood my feelings and asked if he could share another perspective with me.

He suggested, "Cancer cells are ones that have lost their way—lost their identity. These cells are still part of you. The healthy cells that are being affected or threatened need your empathy, strength, and love."

He asked me if I had the psychic space to hate myself. Was self-hate what I wanted to invest my energy in? He asked me to think about where in my life I might have been feeling lost, or in battle.

With the shake-ups, moves, bankruptcy, and other upsets throughout the past year, I had felt very displaced, angry, and lost. It was time to breathe and get present, to remember and embrace how important self-love, laughter, knowledge, and being present are. It was time to find and mobilize my gratitude for this wake-up call called cancer. I would never take life for granted ever again.

I had many conversations with my parents that year about life and death. I told them how terrified I was of dying from cancer because I imagined it to be a very painful process and one that would eat me bit by bit. I told them how scared I was that my youngest son, then five, would not have a chance to get to know me. Might he not remember me in the years to come? It was after discussing and coming to understand the following dream that Jay and I were able to really have conversations with our kids about what was going on with me and explore how they felt.

I dreamed I went to Ari's school to pick him up from pre-k. I parked and went into his classroom. The children were playing at different activity centers with teachers and parent volunteers. Nobody seemed to acknowledge that I had walked in. Nobody said, "Hi." No one smiled or nodded in my direction.

I spoke up to everyone, "Hi, I'm here to get Ari."

No one answered. I tried to speak to each teacher. I walked up to everyone, waving my hands and shouting at them, but I remained unseen and unheard. Slowly parents came to the classroom to pick up their children, and soon Ari was the last one left. By this point, I felt sheer terror and helplessness. And so I ran and screamed at the top of my lungs. I ran so fast and far that soon I was back in our old neighborhood, still screaming, bumping into people, trying to make contact, shake them, push them, but I was invisible. I was dead and gone.

I felt utter hopelessness and dread about the total isolation I imagined in death. I came to think that Ari and his class represented a youthful part of me that was decaying now. Ari and the class also represented my despair that my children would grow up without knowing how much I loved them and that I was always with them.

Jay and my parents helped me to understand that whatever happened, I needed to remember how loved I was and what a wonderful life I was still having. They helped me consider and confront my worst fears. In working through this nightmare and talking endlessly with my loved ones, I came to think that as much as I didn't want to die, I could endure the journey. Somehow I found this acceptable, liberating, and empowering.

Shaving my head was part of the process of accepting and coming to terms with my reality as well. The children could help, and we would make it a memorable ritual.

We explained to each child what we thought they could understand about my cancer, saving the explanation about BRCA until they were much older and could better understand all of the nuances of it. We told Sydney and Eric that I had been diagnosed with cancer at a very early stage and it had been removed through surgery. We told them that I was going to do whatever I could to make sure that it never came back. Among their concerns was that I would lose my hair, and if that happened, wouldn't that mean I was really sick? We explained that it was the opposite. When people having chemo lose their hair, it means that the medicine is working. Hair cells, like cancer cells, grow quickly. The chemo prevents fast cell reproduction, so if hair can't grow, neither—hopefully—can the cancer cells.

My explanation to Ari was much simpler: "I have a boo-boo, Ari, and my doctors are going to make it better. But I have to take yucky medicine." Ari made a face, indicating his understanding of taking yucky medicine. I went on, "My medicine, when it works, might make my tummy hurt, or—here's a funny one…it can make my hair fall out. What do you think of that?"

"Really?"

"Yes, really."

He didn't look happy about that, but also accepted it. He had breastfed until he was almost three and loved playing with my hair as he nursed. Now a few months into being five, he still loved curling up in my lap and twirling my hair in his fingers to soothe himself when he was worried or stressed, and I loved it, too.

Jay and I convened the kids in our bathroom. Sydney had the honor of draping me ceremoniously in a towel. Jay presented me with the scissors, and I made the first cut. Then Jay cut, and each kid took a snip. Sydney and Eric took turns with the video camera and camera. Ari had a special soft brush to keep moving hair off my shoulders and face so I wouldn't itch and sneeze. After the snipping with scissors was done, the buzzer came out. We all watched as I transformed. There was silence now. When it was done, there was a beat of tension.

Then Jay laughed. "Of course…you have a gorgeous, sexy head. Why wouldn't you, when everything else about you is so gorgeous and sexy?"

He gave me a deep, luscious kiss, and the kids smacked their foreheads and groaned.

Eleven-year-old Eric implored, "Oh, gross!"

Then we were all laughing, and we had a tickle-fest, and the shearing of my head was done.

So much, including anxiety about losing my hair, had been about my *fear* of dying. The *actuality* of death, as I was learning, was a separate issue. My belief was that when I die, I'm done. To this day, I don't believe in an afterlife. What I came to see through my experience with cancer was that with my belief that death is the end of the road, there was nothing to fear. There would be no 'me' to be scared.

At the core of it all, I was just really sad imagining my children growing up without me and having to suffer the loss of a parent. I realized that my family and friends might be sad, but they could also understand my wish for them to go on and live their lives. My husband understood this, but the pain I imagined for my children was that which only time and understanding might heal.

Also, there was my dread of missing out on so many wonderful parts of life: weddings, anniversaries, sunrises, grandchildren, and so much more both sacred and mundane. I grieved over the limitations of being human.

As I slowly worked through all of this, the better I felt. I couldn't know how it would all turn out—one never can—but I knew that I was learning about being in the present. I had, and would always have, now. We can have memories of the past and dreams for the future, but the only place we ever really live is in the now. I promised myself that I would aspire to have all my 'nows' register as 'tens' on a scale of one to ten for the rest of my life, as short or long as that might be.

To understand all of this on a molecular level, deep in my gut, confronting my worst fears brought huge relief. I came to see how I had gained perverse benefits from having had cancer. I don't wish to suffer, but out of suffering there can also come profound benefits. Because of this catastrophic illness, I recognized how precious life was.

While I underwent chemotherapy, I created an easy work and parenting schedule for myself. Jay and the parents at Ari's school mobilized incredible support around me and the children. There were always wonderful meals brought to us, and one friend brought us the best homemade banana bread every week. When the kids went to school, I took long, leisurely hikes in the magical hills of Agoura, where I imagined hobbits and elves watching over me from their perches in old oak trees. It made me feel happy to be silly, pretend, and play. I also imagined my grandparents' spirits walking with me, present in the sky and the wind. I learned to take pleasure in my walks, reading, and allowing myself to be taken care of—another perverse benefit of having been sick that I've never forgotten.

A month after I finished with chemotherapy, I had my first of several surgeries. I started with the "simple" outpatient procedure of having my ovaries out, followed a month later with my double mastectomy. By doing this, I decreased the odds of having cancer from almost certainty to almost nothing. I decided to start my breast reconstruction at the same time as the mastectomies. Every six months, when I went in for my blood tests, I worried the cancer had returned, but everything kept coming back clean and clear.

That year, I learned that I had actually inherited my BRCA1 mutation from my father. My results indicated that I had BRCA1, so I couldn't have inherited this from my mother, who also had a BRCA mutation, but it was BRCA2. The distinction between BRCA1 and 2 is, in a broad stroke, that the mutations are located on slightly different spots of the gene and exhibit slightly different characteristics. BRCA1 can only be passed on to a child as BRCA1. My father did get tested, and, sure enough, he had the BRCA1 mutation. At the end of the day, they are both BRCA.

My sisters and Jay also got tested for BRCA. My middle sister tested positive for BRCA1 and 2, and my little sister and Jay thankfully both tested negative. We became proactive, calling family members and encouraging them all, on both sides of the family, to get tested. An interesting outcome was that prior to my having had breast cancer we weren't aware of anyone on my father's side who had had breast or ovarian cancer. They existed, but it had never been openly communicated about. In past generations, open discussion about breast and ovarian cancer had been taboo.

One year after I had been diagnosed with breast cancer, my BRCA-positive sister went in to get pre-operative clearance for preventative surgery. Unfortunately, rather than clearance, her doctor discovered a shadow in her chest x-ray that suggested she might already have breast cancer. This was indeed the case. Cancer and the struggle between life and death and all it brings up continued for another two years in my family, but again, love was our superpower. We came together, talked, supported Amy, went to doctor's visits and chemo, and kept reaching toward life.

Over the next couple years, my sister and I both beat cancer. I opened my own office and went on to get further training as a psychoanalytically trained psychotherapist. My practice started to thrive, and I was in my element, thrilled to be of service and helping people.

I loved my family and work and did not take a single second of time for granted. During that first year of recovery, my hair grew back, and I realized another perverse benefit: I loved my hair super, super short. That definitely never would have been a thing if I hadn't had cancer. Hiking, traveling, learning, peace, and play were all part of my life. I was neither in a hurry nor fearful about moving forward. There were some wonderful ups and some awful downs, but I had developed a powerful context to live my life in.

29
MORE UPS AND DOWNS

E ach of my children had their ups and downs, too. After my cancer, they had some recovery to negotiate as well. Sydney had questions but was very open and resilient. Ari seemed to have accepted that Mommy had had a boo boo and was getting better. Eric seemed the most worried. He had been so caring toward me, and at times angry at his powerlessness when I had been ill. The healthier I became, the more aware I grew of my cancer's emotional effect on Eric. I learned through him that cancer runs deeper and spreads more broadly than just in one person's body.

Quietly, along the road, something had been happening in Eric. The terror and helplessness that he kept locked down while he worried about my frailty and survival came spilling out when he realized I was okay. It was as if he had waited to be sure that I would be sturdy enough to catch his fall.

Jay and I noticed Eric was more and more angry, secretive, and sad. He was always an excellent student, and only a year earlier had led his entire Bar Mitzvah service, which is usually led by the rabbi, on his own. It had been beautiful and so meaningful. I had placed small decorative packs of tissue at everyone's seat, and not an eye was dry by the end. It was extremely emotional as Eric candidly included our dealing with cancer as a family and our road to recovery. I was hopeful that Eric was okay on one level, but at the same time, I knew he wasn't.

Eric had joined the water polo team at his new high school and loved it, but he seemed to be spending less time with old friends. He intensely rejected any involvement Jay or I wanted to have with him.

"Eric, how was school today?"

"Fine, I don't want to talk about it," he'd bark.

"Are you mad at me?" I'd ask.

"Mom, quit trying to be my therapist. God!"

Then he'd storm angrily to his bedroom and disappear into a video game. Some of this, I knew, was normal for a teenager, but when he started slamming doors and seeming more withdrawn, I became much more concerned.

Jay, Eric, and I talked about how sad and angry he seemed and wondered if he was even aware of this. Despite offering very abbreviated and clipped answers, he was aware. We asked Eric whether or not he might want to go to therapy. We shared with him that it felt to us like he'd had an especially painful time during my cancer, and then having recently started high school, with all of its new demands and pressures, it was a lot. We also explained that this would be a lot for anyone, and we all need ways to sort out our difficult thoughts and feelings. He was interested, and he seemed to really like the therapist we found together.

Unfortunately, Eric's pain and anguish ran very deep, and soon he was lying to Jay and me, and lying a lot. We found our money missing, or unauthorized charges on our credit cards. He was purchasing things on the internet, buying video games, clothing items, a little of this and that. Was he buying gifts and trying to impress his friends? Did he feel deprived or like we wouldn't or couldn't give *him* what he really needed? Was he trying to take back something he felt was lost as a result of my illness? We began to attend family therapy sessions with Eric to try and help our beautiful, suffering boy find his way.

There was a turning point at which Eric was so angry and detached, he couldn't seem to speak. No loving word or gesture could reach him. After an extended, worsening time of many months, his therapist, Jay, and I spoke with him about whether he might benefit from a therapeutic boarding school. Still he wouldn't speak. His rage and increasing acting out seemed to be consuming him and our family. Eric seemed not to care about what Ari was exposed to under his influence. He seemed unaware of how sad and hurt Ari could feel. Ari would want to play or spend some time with Eric, and "never" was a good time. Eric pushed Ari away hard. Sydney was baffled and so sad to see her lifelong sibling-comrade slipping away.

With the help of an educational counselor, we learned about a short-term therapeutic wilderness program that might help us initially sort out and assess what was going on with Eric. From there, he would go on to a therapeutic boarding school for gifted young people. Jay and I were bitterly torn and felt bereft. When we were in a room with Eric, he seemed utterly absent—gone. Our hearts were breaking, and we couldn't reach him. We could only imagine that if he continued to spiral down the path he was on that he would wind up in jail or dead. But at the same time, how could we let him go? What kind of mother would that make me if I "sent him away"? All of us felt tortured.

On a cold November morning, when Eric was only fourteen, Jay woke Eric up and told Eric he wanted to take him to look at a boarding school. That was not true. He was taking him on a plane to Utah to a therapeutic wilderness program, but we had been advised not to discuss the nature of the first leg of his journey. He wasn't to pack or prepare. He left bringing only his wallet with him. Eric did not resist and was compliant, but he was steely and icy in his attitude. I hugged his stiff body with mighty tenderness, love and tears in my eyes. When he walked out the door, taking a piece of my heart with him, I had no idea if the drastic measures we had decided on were right or not.

Eric backpacked for the next ten weeks with a handful of other boys and some counselors. He carried a primitive wooden backpack he had crafted as part of the program. There were no cell phones and no computers. As they trekked through the internal badlands of their minds, it became evident that how they negotiated the wilderness around them was an apt metaphor for their life journeys. Eric received individual and group therapy, guidance, survival training, and an unforgettable life transformation there. At the end of the wilderness program, he soloed for a couple days, and that was when Jay and I were able to reunite with him.

Eric had made a bullroarer, an ancient musical instrument that was also used for communicating over great distances as far back as 5,000 BCE in Scandinavia and countries throughout the world. It's a simple wooden disc at the end of a chord, and when it's swung overhead, it makes a buzzing sound, loud and resonant. Jay and I were given a bullroarer, and we were to listen for Eric's bullroarer. We were in the middle of nowhere in a beautiful, silent, snowy desert. As we walked, too nervous to be cold, choked up, listening intently, we heard his 'hum.' We listened to each other's sounds and gravitated closer to one another, one step at a time. Then, there he was. Eric was caked in dirt, his hair had grown into matted dreadlocks, and his eyes sparkled and gleamed with clarity, love, and tremendous joy. Eric was smiling and crying. He had come back to himself.

We nearly knocked each other over when we plunged into each other's arms. Eric cooked a wonderful meal for us over a fire that he kindled with his flint stone. It was the best corn masa I'd ever had, with hot herbal tea. We exchanged some small talk, laughed, and snuggled. We talked about my cancer, his helplessness, our helplessness, his fears about opening up, his anger, hurt, and understanding about having been left in the wilderness of his program but also in his life. He was happy, he was sad, and he was able to talk about it all. I could write a whole book about just this episode, but that's for another time. For now, what's important is that Eric was returning to himself. It was so painful at times. I felt like I was the worst parent in the world sending my sweet baby away, but that was my selfishness, wanting to keep him close and also not wanting to look bad to him, my family, or friends. Ultimately, I knew we were on the right path to healing and repair, but still it didn't make leaving him at his boarding school any easier.

Eric spent one and a half years at his school. We visited him for therapeutic weekends, and alternately, as he got stronger and clearer, he came home for visits. There was work that the school had us do as a family, that Jay and I had to do as parents, and that Eric did every day he was there. As much as I ached for Eric when he was away, I believe the education, therapy, friendships, and attention he received at his school helped him profoundly and may have saved his life.

As Eric's access to his feelings, truth, openness, and ability to think about his experiences developed, it became clear that he *wanted* to come home. And he did. He had a deeply touching culmination ceremony at the school, then came home for his senior year of high school. He went to a local school he wasn't crazy about but made friends, fell in love, and was himself. He engaged with Jay and me about his fiery hopes and dreams. He was angry that he'd had to be away, but understood that he'd made gains that were undeniably life altering.

There would be more ups and downs along the way. But always, we come back to love. We come back to understanding. I guess there exists an invisible bullroarer that supersedes the difficulties and pains we encounter and pulls us back to family.

I was alive. I was there to see Eric and Ari become B'nai Mitzvah. I was there to fight with them over curfew and rules about driving and screen time. I was able to send them to sleep-away camp and miss them. Sydney and Eric graduated from high school, and I laughed and cried when we dropped them off at the airport to take their gap years in Israel. I was able to celebrate and worry and celebrate again.

30
ONE MORE THING...MAMMA

As I approached my fiftieth birthday, a few significant things happened. I had completed the Team, Management, and Leadership Program (TMLP) at Landmark Education a year earlier, and the coach of the course put concisely into words an idea I had been trying to give shape to: "We are always either expanding or contracting as human beings."

If we give into the default of being human, it's pretty predictable that we will lean toward complacency and, rather than expand, find ourselves contracting, taking life for granted. We tend to want to expand only if we are conscious of the value we have for life.

Recently, I was listening to a podcast of Hal Elrod's, whose chief commitment in life is to raise the consciousness of human beings everywhere, one person at a time. He was talking about our inherited primitive inclinations from early human experience. He explained that when we were hungry and out of food, the instinct for life and self-preservation kicked in. We hunted down bison or elk, requiring a great deal of work and ingenuity. Then we would do the work of preparing the meat and feeding our family or tribe. Finally, we could hang out, eat, sleep, and watch the clouds float by until the next food shortage or existential threat presented itself.

I recognized my existential hunger. I recognized the importance of getting out and continuing the hunt, expanding, or I might contract and stop really being conscious of how precious life is. For me, the hunt has always involved the desire to make a difference for others. I recognized my desire to pursue a doctorate in psychoanalysis and again raise the bar on my skill and capacity to help people.

I hunted down the right program for me and sorted out the time commitment with Jay and Ari, the two folks still left at home with me. Sydney was in college, and Eric away in Israel—two down. I asked Ari how he felt about us doing homework together, and he thought it was pretty cool.

It was a rigorous program that focused on primitive or baby mental states. The premise was that we don't ever leave the 'baby us' behind. The 'baby us' is always contributing to or detracting from our ability to grow, succeed, and take pleasure in life. This is often done unconsciously. Psychoanalysis is about helping people access their unconscious parts, of which the baby part is only one, and to access communication and feeling within all areas of our mental life. The academic portion of the program was four years, plus cases that needed to be followed clinically under the supervision of advanced analysts, while also undergoing a personal analysis, and culminated with a final paper. One of the distinguishing and important factors of doing psychoanalysis as distinct from psychotherapy is the fact that you are seen four to five times a week. So I was asking for a large commitment from my family and of myself.

A few months into beginning this rigorous and exciting program, I received a call from my parents. My mother, who had had her ovaries removed twenty years earlier, before BRCA had been a known entity in our family, had been diagnosed with ovarian cancer. Apparently when she'd had the surgery preventatively years earlier, the surgeon did not remove her fallopian tubes. The tubes are comprised of the same cells that are found in the ovaries. We also have "ovarian cells" in the omentum, a part of the abdomen. I now know that even with the removal of the fallopian tubes, there is always some risk of ovarian-type cancer. Mom had a fluid-filled tumor that required removal, and if it were to break while still in her body, cancerous cells would spread everywhere.

My mother found a remarkable surgeon, who, despite it being a very tough surgery, was able to remove the tumor intact. Ten years later, my mother is still alive and well and beat the grim odds against her. I can't help but think that again, this was helped by state of mind and mental attitude. With so many risk factors and frightening experiences, it is easy to be fatalistic, but I am convinced that the key to living a successful life includes accepting life as is. We all eventually get to the end of the road, and it is most important to be present and enjoy the journey. It was hard to include all the pain and worry when my mom was undergoing surgery and treatment for her cancer while focusing on my studies, and yet that was what there was to do.

Meanwhile, Sydney thrived in college, and in the midst of her studies, met the love of her life, Brit. What's funny is that the girls knew each other in high school and befriended each other on their gap years in Israel, but didn't become romantically involved until much later. Jay and I loved Brit and how the two young women loved each other. After their graduation, Sydney started her social media and public relations company with Brit, and shortly thereafter, they proposed to each other and became engaged.

After being stationed in the military in North Carolina, Eric decided he wanted to come back home again, complete college, and pursue a career in law. Ari had begun high school and excelled in the theater program and played on the school's football team. As he became clearer that his passion was in acting, that became his focus. And on the final frontier, Jay's practice had become full and an important presence in our community, particularly with Homeless Not Toothless flourishing. Everyone was in action and on the path, immersed deeply in life.

31

ARI FALLS DOWN, BUT HE GETS UP AGAIN AND AGAIN— LEARNING FROM MY CHILDREN

Ari was growing up fast. His sixteenth summer came, and he wanted to go on a youth group mission to Ecuador, where he would teach English to children there, help build a school, and develop his Spanish speaking abilities. While there and loving it, he had a massive seizure on the Inca Trail in the middle of nowhere at 15,000 feet of elevation. He had never had a seizure before. The camp verified it, but also said that the satellite phone they used to communicate with the counselors was down for the night and they wouldn't be able to clarify anything further until the morning. They said that he was at such high elevation, and oxygen was so thin that they had to wait until morning to hike him down to base camp and get him to the nearest major hospital, a teaching hospital in Cuenca, Ecuador.

I flew to Ari as quickly as possible, not at all happy that he still had to backpack off the mountain. Within twenty-four hours, I was with him, met his wonderful host family, and spoke to the specialist who had seen him and started him on anti-seizure medications. This doctor was lovely but firm and unequivocal in his diagnosis. He said we needed to return home and see a specialist as soon as possible.

We would learn over the following weeks that Ari had epilepsy. Ari was worked up inside and out. Epilepsy is diagnostically and prognostically vague, and its remission is indicated only by lack of seizures and time. Medication and lifestyle adjustments are the mainstay of prevention. For Ari, this meant no driving, plenty of rest, good nutrition, and as he got older, minimal to no alcohol. After he came home from Ecuador and had been on his medications for a few weeks, he was overcome by the wish to deny and rebel against his diagnosis.

Ari "missed" a few doses of medication, and early on a Sunday morning, Jay and I heard, *thump, thump, thump, thump, thump* in quick, loud succession. We ran to the bottom of the stairs, and there was Ari, thrashing, salivating, rigid—then slumping. He passed out. It was a horror. There was nothing we could do as it was happening other than keep his head from pounding our stone floors. His brain was misfiring, and his body had hijacked him. When he came to, he didn't know who or where he was. He didn't know who Jay was, or who I was. His speech was slurred, jumbled, and halting. We called 911, and they were on their way.

Because we now lived in Malibu Canyon, which is under constant firewatch, there was a firehouse minutes away from us. It felt like they arrived before we even hung up the phone. They in turn reached out for backup because it was clear Ari had fallen down the flight of stairs, and we didn't know the extent of damage he might have suffered from the trauma. An additional team showed up and airlifted us to UCLA Emergency in Westwood. A drive that could have taken us more than an hour under normal circumstances we made in minutes by helicopter. Ari was badly bumped and bruised, but his body would recover quickly, and there was no permanent damage. The lack of recognition and memory Ari experienced when he first became conscious can be typical post-seizure, and is only short-lasting. The more serious damage was to his confidence, pride, and sense of normalcy. We have learned over the years, and after numerous seizures, that Ari has been blessed with great resilience and a hard head, quite literally.

Ari struggled to find his legs as an independent young man, as adolescents must, yet had to do this while not knowing when and if he might have a major seizure. He is creative, smart, loving, sensitive, and funny. He is an actor and comedian, writer, and fitness coach. He has had periods without seizures, and then periods where he can't get through a year without multiple, but he always gets up again. I believe, again and still, that love is the superpower behind Ari's will and strength. I know he has felt terribly afraid, angry, sad, and cheated. It doesn't feel fair. It is, however, the undeniable reality, and he has chosen to look at it head-on, cope, and live his life fully. He has allowed the love of his family and community in, and has also developed self-love. I love learning from him.

As Ari adjusted to his health challenges, he made his way impressively through high school. In his senior year, he was accepted to his first choice fine arts acting college in New York. There were only twenty-something students accepted to the freshman class. I was thrilled for Ari, but also terrified of letting him go so far away when we had such a tenuous hold on his seizures.

He came to me one afternoon while I was making dinner. He seemed excited and reported to me that there was a girl who he had known in ninth grade who had also been accepted to his program. He had reached out to her, hopeful they could be friends at school. I think we both felt a little relieved that he already knew someone. In fact, I remembered that she had been his "date" for his fourteenth birthday party.

Shortly after Ari reached out to her about college, I received a message from the girl's mother. She said that she needed to talk to me urgently. Concerned and busy, after calling unsuccessfully a couple of times, I asked Jay if he could follow up because I didn't want to drop the ball. This mom seemed worried. Jay called and got through to the girl's father. What followed was shocking and unthinkable.

The girl's father told us that Ari needed to withdraw his acceptance to college, because otherwise his daughter would press charges against Ari for raping her in ninth grade. Jay was floored and completely blindsided. This was crazy. Not only is Ari gentle and respectful, but we were right there, supervising every minute of the one and only visit between them. There was no rape, assault, or weird contact. Of course, despite what we felt we already knew, we had to ask Ari directly.

"Did you rape her?"

Ari went ashen. "Are you crazy?"

We told him about the phone call. Ari was upset and angry and hurt. One moment, he cried and the next banged a fist on the table. "How is this even happening? What does this even mean? Why is she saying this?"

When Jay got back to the father and told him that he was sure there must be some misunderstanding, the father became enraged, reiterated the ultimatum, and hung up. Jay came to me and recounted what had happened. Again, I reached out to the mother of the girl. I left a rather long and detailed message: "I understand that there is a dreadful misunderstanding between our children. Maybe we can get together and talk things out, really get to the bottom of this. I'm sure you feel terrible, but I'm also sure that my son never assaulted your daughter. I was right there the whole time, with my husband. Why don't we talk and see if we can help the kids get through whatever this is?"

The next message we got was in the form of a subpoena. Ari was served to show up at criminal court in Santa Monica. The girl wanted a restraining order, including an order prohibiting Ari from attending their mutual school. This had gotten scary and disturbing fast. We shared what was going on with our family and friends. We were connected through referrals to an attorney who believed Ari and took the case. The girl didn't show up to the first hearing, and the case was dismissed. We thought it was over. We were very wrong.

Ari received a second subpoena. This time it was from family court, and again it was a request for a restraining order. We met with our two attorneys who were on this case. Ari was interviewed by them alone and again with me and Jay, and was then asked to send every document he had that showed communication between him and the girl. At the time, we thought we had to act quickly before this girl started erasing evidence. What we have since learned is that once you publish anything online it never disappears.

At this point, family and friends who love us all were advising us to drop this, and suggested that maybe Ari would want to go to one of his backup schools. We did talk about it, but he didn't want this to linger unfinished, forever a possible threat in his life. He hadn't done anything wrong, and he wasn't going to let it go. Jay, Sydney, Eric, Brit (who was already part of the family), and I were entirely supportive of Ari.

Brit and Sydney, masters of social media, started scouring Facebook and found pages and pages of communication between Ari and the girl both before and after the alleged assault. All the communications were friendly. At one point, it was clear that the girl kept reaching out and Ari was trying to disengage. She was very persistent.

The kids received a court date two weeks before their freshman year was to start. The hearing lasted three days. The girl's behavior was bizarre. On the first day, in the corridor, she calmly whispered to her mother, giggled, and seemed fine, but then she would flip a switch and burst into loud tears. In the courtroom, she vacillated between being overly sweet with the judge and raging at him.

By day three, several things had become clear. This girl was having a hard time. My sister Amy was the senior vice-president of Intensive Intervention Programs at Vista Del Mar, a comprehensive mental health organization that provides care for children and their families in Los Angeles. As Amy observed this girl over the first two days of the court proceedings, she told me she had the feeling that the girl had endured terrible suffering and was indeed in pain. Although my heart went out to her, blaming Ari was a terrible displacement—a dark, cruel, sadistic stab.

At the end of the second day, the judge explained that if we pursued this further, the next court date would interfere with the start of their schooling. He asked the girl if she would be willing to drop the case, and she cried inconsolably, shaking visibly, claiming she couldn't. The judge explained that the findings could go one of three ways. First, the case could be found to be without merit and be thrown out. Second, Ari could be found guilty and would have a formal temporary restraining order drawn up. Or third, the girl would be found in contempt and she could be fined and wind up being the one with the restraining order. He recommended that we agree to disagree. The girl, her father, and counsel reluctantly agreed to mediation.

The mediation took half a day. Both parties agreed to keep their distance, but apparently Ari had agreed to an unofficial restraining order against him. The temporary restraining order, or TRO, wasn't entered in the national criminal database, but it meant he had to be the one who left a room if he went somewhere and the girl was there. They agreed that the dean would be worked with, and she would arrange for them to have separate classes. When it was impossible for them to exit a room, they would remain as far apart as possible. The onus was ultimately on Ari.

The agreement we signed was that Ari and the girl would keep their distance from each other for their four years at the college or until one of them left. If one left, the agreement would be dissolved. They also both agreed that it would be a violation of the agreement to discuss the case with anyone. The agreement was not an admission of guilt for either of them, but rather, the mediating judge said, "This is an agreement that you have agreed to disagree."

Both kids began school as planned. Jay and I had a wonderful experience bringing Ari to New York, meeting his roommate and some of the kids in his program. We all went to orientations and took Ari out for some memorable meals. The day came when we had to leave, and he seemed to be in a really good place. It was so tough for me to walk away from my last child.

A week later, Jay and I reached out to Ari to wish him a happy birthday. He sobbed. All the kids in his program had approached him and asked what he was doing at their school and why he had raped this girl. She had broken the mediation agreement and shared the whole story from her point of view, that Ari had allegedly raped her in high school at our home, with anyone who would listen. She expressed that after being raped she had been terrified of Ari. She said she had been in therapy extensively and cut herself repeatedly. She said that she had been so traumatized that there had been no other boyfriends afterward.

Ari was humiliated and felt helpless. He knew it wouldn't go well if he broke the agreement, and could only respond with, "I'm sorry, but I can't talk about it." He couldn't even say why he couldn't talk about it. He was excluded and ostracized. Although we spoke with our attorney, there wasn't much we could do. Our attorney did reach out to the girl's attorney, and he made clear to her what was going on and that her client needed to cease and desist, but the damage was done.

As the next year and a half unfolded, Ari went to class, did his work, and stayed away from the girl. The girl, it seemed, was known by the dean and security officers because she regularly showed up at their offices with photos of the back of Ari's head. She would show these photos and complain that he was following her and threatening her, when clearly she was coming up from behind him and taking pictures. One day toward the end of freshmen year, Ari was in the dining hall in his dorm. He was in his pajamas, eating breakfast, and hanging out with his friends. At some point, the girl came in, saw him, and posted a threatening Snapchat stating something to the effect of, "I'll show him." She went to the front of the building and called 911. She told the dispatcher that she was being harassed by a boy who she had a restraining order against. Ari hadn't even seen her.

School security guards came to Ari where he sat with his friends and asked him to please go with them. When he got to the security office, there were two policemen waiting. Without any introduction, they jumped right in and asked him why he had been harassing the girl. Ari was shocked. He told them he hadn't been aware she was even there. He said he was just having breakfast with friends.

"Yeah, sure, we've heard that before. Get up."

Before Ari knew what was happening, he was roughly handcuffed, ankle-shackled, and perp-walked through the school in front of everybody. He saw that the situation was hopeless, but implored the policemen that he had epilepsy and needed his meds. They dismissed his complaint and dragged him away in his slippers. To say this was devastating is an understatement. The girl's sadism was out of control, and Ari was clearly at the epicenter of her rage.

Ari received the privilege of a single outgoing call once he got to the precinct. He called Jay, who was stunned but also super pissed. We had played nice all along, but this was just too far. Jay called the school and talked to the security office, who told Jay that they thought "this girl is nuts. She's always in here bringing us weird pictures that show Ari at a distance, or show the back of his head at a distance. She's in here a few times a week."

By spring, she had made over fifty complaints against Ari and opened up a Title IX discrimination case against him at school. The dean had investigated and found Ari to be an innocent bystander. There had been one instance where the dean hadn't been clear about who arrived first to the site of complaint, so she wasn't sure how to rule, but otherwise she found that Ari consistently upheld the settlement agreements.

We were referred to another lawyer in New York, a criminal attorney. After reviewing the case, he was eager to help. He acquired the closed-circuit footage from school that showed Ari relaxing in the cafeteria, minding his own business. The lawyer showed up at Ari's arraignment the following morning. When the judge saw the school security footage, he immediately dismissed Ari's case. Ari had been in jail overnight and missed two doses of medication. It was soon after this that Ari had his first seizure at school. He fell down a flight of stairs, lost a tooth, and bruised his whole body. By the start of the following year, Ari had another seizure on the streets in New York, and he woke up with his wallet and phone gone, again bruised head to toe and with a whopping case of amnesia.

One day, Jay had a fairly new patient in his chair. She had heard about Jay because of his work with the homeless. She was an attorney who, in her spare time, devoted herself to the rights of immigrants, particularly those fleeing Yemen through Djibouti. Jay and she clicked. As they got to talking, she became very interested in Ari's story. She wanted every detail. Then, she wanted to meet him, and when she got back to New York she did just that.

She wanted the case. She felt Ari hadn't been properly defended. It wasn't that our attorneys had been 'bad'; they just weren't good for Ari. Our new attorney was furious and felt Ari had been abused, maltreated, and that even the restraining order against him was "illegal." Wow! I liked her a lot. She really wanted to help, and we really wanted her help. She immediately filed cases and a number of news agencies caught wind of her fury. The story was published in a variety of places, including several New York newspapers and on Facebook feeds. Although Ari still kept his agreement as per the settlement and said nothing about the case, Ari's friends crawled out of the woodwork in his support and defense. Superpower love to the rescue!

Within a couple of months, we were back in an L.A. courtroom. Our attorney had moved to have the initial agreement thrown out and a formal restraining order permanently obtained against the girl. We contacted Ari's neurologist, therapist, school officials, and we subpoenaed documents. When the judge in Covina heard opening arguments, he realized that this was serious and not a slam-dunk case. Again, the girl was there with her father and attorney. Ari came with a huge entourage. As the days wore on, friends and family joined us and offered support in the gallery or hallways.

Both young people were called to testify. The girl's leaky eyes and grand gestures had no positive effect on this judge. He seemed annoyed and put off by her distractions. At one point, she was caught in a lie and wanted to plead the fifth amendment. The judge explained that if she wanted to do that she could, but then she would not be allowed any further testimony at all. Eventually, she succumbed and talked herself in circles. She said she hadn't seen Ari again after being allegedly raped.

"Definitely not," she said emphatically.

She testified under oath that she had not erased any posts on Facebook or social media that might be seen as incriminating. Everything was as it was and had been for years, she said. She gave dates, then changed dates. It was hard to tell the lies from the truth. She and her attorney had no corroborating documentation or experts to testify on the girl's behalf.

Having worked at the Santa Monica Rape Treatment Center, I am sensitive to the fact that often victims of rape don't file reports or go to hospitals because they are so traumatized. But this young woman alleged that she *had* gone with her mother to the police and to the hospital. She had told us in our first court appearance and then again in these hearings of how she had been in therapy. Despite this testimony, no reports to police of a rape were produced as evidence, there was no record of a hospital visit produced as evidence, and no therapist or expert were brought in on her behalf, either. There were many strange and ever-changing stories and details. Equally as disruptive was the constant tardiness of the girl's counsel. Not once did her attorney show up on time.

Among our difficulties during those hearings was that many of our documents were denied by the court because of the rushed nature of their acquisition. There was a chain of evidence that had to be followed, and much of what we had, including the video in the cafeteria, was inadmissible. Ari's therapist was able to testify as an expert, and he was able to testify to Ari's character, state of mind, and the link between his stress, feelings of being unjustly and publicly punished, and his increased seizure activity.

On the fourth day, the judge asked if he could see the Facebook posts—the actual posts. Our attorney explained that the girl had erased everything that was damning to her, but if he gave us until the following day, we could provide the evidence he was asking for. He agreed. As a family on November 6, 2017, we composed a Facebook post:

"Hi all… I am asking for some help from my Facebook community.

I desperately need to speak to somebody who is a Facebook executive or founder that might be able to help me with a current problem I am having. I am in court on behalf of a family member who many of you know and love, and awful accusations are being made. However, the truth could surface if we had access to posts and messages on Facebook that have been deleted. If we don't gain access by tomorrow, 8:30 am Pacific time, this may turn into a very lengthy, messy process, and I believe all sides will suffer terribly. Please message me if you or someone you know might be able to help…"

Then we added a note specifically addressed to the people we had come to know in the Team, Management, and Leadership Program Jay and I had been in. There is a general commitment by all who filter through this program to integrity, love, and working together as a team. Every goal and accomplishment in this program is moved forward through the structure of a formal "game." So following is the "game" we created that night.

"TMLPers:

We have created a [game of] possibility [with an] outcome [and] measurable results:

The Possibility: being present, loving, playful, whole, and complete.

The Outcome: everyone who plays wins in whatever they are committed to, and has the bliss of integrity with freedom and ease.

Results now: truth emerges; information is easily made available.

Tomorrow is our last day in court.

Please contact me now and through tonight.

The game is to locate a Facebook executive who wants to help us and believes us.

The game ends tomorrow morning at 8:30 when we walk back into court."

Each of us posted this game and message, and the responses were overwhelming. The TMLPers wanted to play. At ten o'clock that night, someone we knew who had worked in the administration at Landmark Education, the educational institution that offers the TMLP, reached out to Jay. He assured us that he knew our family and the work we do in the community. This person had been employed at Facebook. He wasn't able to get to the courthouse the next day, but he was able to tell us how to access and read the code that gets you behind the scenes to see every post a person has made on their account—whether it has been publicly erased or not.

We still needed an expert to corroborate what we had learned. Our lead attorney's second chair had a friend in cyber-security whose credentials were off the chart. He had worked in social media, major news networks, and had contracts with the government.

Not only was he interested, but he also told us how easily he could show a judge who had no computer skills how to navigate this himself. He was all in. We are forever grateful.

The next day, we were sitting in the halls, having been cast out of the courtroom. The judge didn't want any parental influence in his court while the kids were testifying. We saw a character in baggy jeans sporting some very visible tattoos, looking a little intimidating, ambling toward us. He was the one. We talked a little bit with the expert, and then we let our attorney know that he was there. Soon enough, he was called in. We hoped he wouldn't be pre-judged on appearances alone— never judge a book by its cover!

The expert made good on his promise and walked the judge through the process of accessing the code on the back side of Facebook. The judge was able to see every post the girl had made. He was able to see how much she had reached out to Ari and how frequently she had altered the timeline and the truth about dates. There was to be a lunch recess, the attorneys would compose their closing remarks, and then the judge would rule.

We allowed the girl and her parents to leave for lunch before we went out. We had made a practice of trying to give them space and privacy between court sessions. Ari, Jay, Sydney, Brit, Eric, and our two attorneys were sitting together, huddled, quarterbacking the previous moments and anticipating what the judge might be thinking. Suddenly, we heard screaming. We went running up the hallway to the bank of elevators, where the parents were yelling at their daughter.

"You told us you hid everything!"

"I did!" she cried back at them.

She looked as though she was receiving a beating.

Her parents were merciless and unrelenting, "Well, clearly you didn't. You've really screwed this up!" they yelled. The girl was red and crying. It felt violently intimate, and none of us knew what to do or say. I felt truly sad for her.

There was still an hour to wait while our attorney composed her closing remarks and the judge did his deliberating, but there had been a definite shift in everyone's moods. We finally felt optimistic that we could get to the other side of this.

We returned early to the courtroom. We were eager and nervous. The girl, her family, and her attorney returned late. The judge listened again, nodding, shaking his head, and making notes. The suspense was killing us. Then it was his turn. He recapped the entire five-day trial. It seemed to take forever, and it was hard to tell where he was leading us. Finally, he offered, "I have come to a judgment."

He was clear about how extensive the girl's lies had been. She did not try to change her story and say that there had been some other incident with Ari besides when she had been at our home under our supervision. This made it even more difficult for the judge to believe that the girl could have been raped, when Jay and I had our parental eyes on the two kids for their whole visit. Finally, he went through the timeline and used the girl's own posts and messages as a guideline. He was furious. Ari was vindicated, and the restraining order against him was to be removed. The girl was to be issued a TRO for the next year, at which point, if we renewed it, it would convert to a permanent and nationally recognized restraining order.

All Ari wanted was to get back to school, where he had been missing crucial classes, and walk with his head held high. Our attorney got him on a flight, first class. What an ordeal. Within days, the girl packed her bags and left school. We celebrated with family and friends and acknowledged our formal and informal teammates from the Team, Management, and Leadership Program.

Unfortunately for Ari, so much damage had already been done. There were still so many kids in his year who just couldn't forgive him. Ari was living off campus with a self-absorbed roomate. He felt lonely and was having seizures. He was struggling to cope. At the end of that year, he reached out and recognized that he needed family support and wanted to come home. The nugget of gold is that, once home, Ari wasn't left in his despondency and anxiety alone. He was able to talk about his need for family support to progress forward.

When Ari returned home, he was able to work more intimately with his neurologist. The neurologist helped Ari understand that being in an environment with reduced stress and where he could see his doctor and track his medication more closely would significantly help his seizures. His doctor also helped him understand that his active seizures were not likely to be a part of his life forever. Today, Ari continues to work hard as he figures out his path as an actor while building his business as a personal trainer, and I am very proud of him.

For each moment of success and joy we encountered during this period, we also experienced the hard impact of illness, accident, or insanity. Living a full and happy life does not mean living a life that doesn't include hardship, pain, and loss. These difficult dark times bring perverse benefits, opportunities for growth and learning, and even joy. If we digest them thoughtfully, with love and with our eyes on our greater commitments, it all comes together to make for a wonderful life.

It was the drive to live and love that gave me inspiration, courage, and context. Underpinnings are placed throughout childhood and our teen years. Strength and determination are built further in adult relationships, marriage, and work. Love, laughter, and the ability to be in the moment are so important. Life is a creative process and requires profound commitment, especially in the face of adversity, fear, and apathy. When life is easy and seems to be going our way, it may not require a great deal of difficult work, but when it is difficult, that's when we are pressed to rally and access our foundation of love to recognize that perverse benefits will eventually be reaped.

VII

SILVER LININGS: MAGIC MOMENTS WILL ALWAYS COME, GIVEN TIME

"Still round the corner there may wait,
a new road or a secret gate."
—J.R.R. TOLKEIN (1892-1973)
BRITISH AUTHOR, POET, PHILOLOGIST, ACADEMIC

32
WEDDING BELLS

Let's backtrack a little bit. It became clear to everyone that Sydney and Brit were b'sheret, just like Jay and me. In fact, I remember when Sydney first came to me and told me that Brit had asked her out on a date. She told me that she really liked Brit, and wanted to know how I felt about this. I told her she should follow her heart.

Four years later, both girls graduated from college having studied communication and journalism. Jay and I engaged in lively conversations as we imagined what might be next for them. The more they worked and played together, the clearer it became to anyone who knew them how deeply they loved each other and how powerful they could be when they worked together. Everything they set their minds to they put extraordinary effort into. They learned from their experiences of building teams, management, and becoming leaders that one must work through the inevitable tough and confronting times to relish the journey and accomplishment. They were thriving.

We all know that they wound up together, but some of the details are important here.

Valentine's Day has become a significant holiday in our family, and it was on that day in 2015 that Brit and Sydney surprised us on a beach in Malibu. It was wonderful. Jay and I had escaped to a lovely inn to share some quiet loving time together. We wined and dined, had great conversation, and relaxed.

On Sunday morning, we were lying on the beach, relaxing, sharing the Sunday *L.A. Times.* We heard a little voice calling, "Mommy, Mommy."

I said, "How sweet. Remember when our children were little, calling for us on the beach?"

The voice got louder, and I saw two figures leaping up the beach.

"Honey, honey, is that Sydney...and...Brit?" I asked Jay.

Why would they be here when they knew we wanted alone time for Valentine's Day?

The girls were giddy with happiness. Sydney was approaching me now with her hands held out. The girls were laughing, their faces beaming. They had proposed to each other and accepted each other's proposal. They were jumping up and down, and their love and enthusiasm were absolutely contagious.

The girls were married a year later. We had many conversations about the varied reactions they received when they announced their engagement and throughout the year of their engagement. Most people were thrilled for them, but every once in a while they met hostility and pushback that two women cannot "really" marry each other. What I saw in my girls back then, these smart loving young women, was their courage and strength.

In one conversation, Syd and Brit wanted some input from me and Jay about their honeymoon destination. They had wanted to go to a tropical, exotic, far-away Shangri-La. What they encountered were reviews about many of those spots where LGBT couples were met with prejudice, cruelty, and sometimes danger and violence. In a conversation with them, I recommended Maroma, in the Mayan Peninsula.

"It will feel exotic, the beaches are beautiful, and it's a wonderfully warm and accepting community," I suggested.

They did some research on their own. I will never forget Brit approaching me, holding Sydney's hand with a Cheshire Cat smile on her face.

"Oh my God! It's beautiful—and they were so welcoming when we spoke with them." Brit eagerly continued, "We are going to Maroma. But just one thing…. Do you and Jay want to join us? You guys are so great to travel with. Why don't you join us?!"

I was moved by the offer. "Brit, Sydney, I love that you would want Jay and me to celebrate with you; however, there are some things you gotta do on your own. I'm thinking that your honeymoon is one of them!"

There was a pause in the conversation, and we all broke out laughing.

When they finally took their vows, it had been less than a year since same-sex marriage had become legal nationally. It was an amazing celebration of their love and of their freedom to love. They incorporated many traditional Jewish customs to their wedding and also added their own personal touch. Sydney wore the veil I had worn twenty-nine years earlier, and both girls dressed in white, flowing gowns. They looked like they would float away on the ether of the day. There was laughing and crying. There were tears and joy as we danced and made toasts. Multiple generations, family, and friends came together to experience the wedding in community. Love wins again.

33
BABIES ANYONE?

S ydney, like her mother, knew from a young age that she wanted to grow up and become a mother herself. She loved her brothers, dollies, and Beanie Babies from the very beginning. She also was enamored by the videos I showed in my childbirth classes. She especially seemed to love the class reunions where she saw the pregnant mommies come back with their babies in their arms. Brit also wanted babies, but wasn't as sure about whether she wanted to carry a baby, or how this would all work.

They had some choices to make. They decided Sydney would carry. Then they had to think about whose sperm would be donated for insemination. They could have used Brit's brothers' sperm, but they weren't comfortable that the babies' uncle would also be the biological father. They thought about possibly asking a friend, but ruled that out also. Instead, they researched some sperm banks. They chose one and began looking at donor profiles to figure out what characteristics were important to them that might most express the attributes of each of them, regardless of who was carrying. They considered blood type, hair and eye color, and health history. After exhaustive research, they chose "in bulk." They figured out the who and the how and that they wanted enough sperm from one donor to have four children. And so it was done.

Sydney had a small window in which she was most fertile. Brit was at work when the time came, so Sydney asked me if I wanted to go with her for her IUI (intrauterine insemination). I felt deeply privileged. The doctor was very supportive and encouraging. We were aware impregnation could take a few tries, but there's no harm in wishing. I held Sydney's hand as the doctor inserted the sperm. Then it was a waiting game.

A month later was the Jewish holiday of Passover. I was going to have a large ceremonial meal at my house and needed to do a lot of grocery shopping. My cart was full, and I was just about ready to check out, but wanted to grab some festive flowers for my tables. I looked up from a bunch of sunflowers and couldn't quite make sense of what I was seeing: Sydney and Brit...in matching T-shirts. Wait, what did the shirts say? There were cartoons of a mother, mother, dog, and baby, and it said, "And Then There Were Four."

I couldn't help myself from crying and laughing and declaring over and over, "Oh my God, oh my God, you're pregnant! You are really pregnant!" I think I had the whole damn market celebrating. The girls were delirious, too. Sydney had just gotten the news that morning and went to work immediately making the T-shirts. That's how she told Brit when Brit got home, and that's how both of them told Jay, myself, and Brit's parents, too. It was amazing.

34
THE PAST IS PRESENT

That first week was full of excitement and sharing with family. Everyone was thrilled for Sydney and Brit; it was a time of celebration and happy anticipation. My phone rang as I was getting ready to go home from the office one day, and I saw it was my youngest sister calling. I was eager to gab with her about how excited we both were about the new baby.

Laura said, "Hi," tentatively, followed with, "I have a question for you."

"Great, go ahead," I said, upbeat.

"Well, are you sitting down? I think you should probably just sit down for a minute."

She sounded a little funny, and I assured her that I was indeed sitting.

"Okay," she pushed on. "I just had an interesting conversation with my poodle breeder. She told me that her friend lives in Missouri, and has a brother-in-law nearby who is a donor baby. His dad passed away a year ago, and he took the 23andMe online genetic test to see if he could locate his biological dad. He wondered about his genetic health, since his dad died of cancer. He happened to be following a thread on the poodle group that led to me, and *that* led, ultimately, to Jay. Is it possible that Jay is this guy's biological dad?"

Apparently, this young man had been trying to reach Jay through the messaging app on 23andMe, where Jay also had a profile, but Jay had done the test years earlier and, having found nothing remarkable, stopped receiving email updates. He hadn't checked it in years.

I started to laugh. "Yes, it's possible, and not unlikely."

I told Laura about Jay's being a sperm donor when we were in graduate school. I told her I was going to head home soon, but maybe she could call him right then. She agreed, but first told me the young man's name and that I should see his pictures on Facebook. She said he looked just like Jay, and he did.

After Jay spoke with Laura, and before speaking with me, he found himself in shock. He told Sydney and Brit what had happened, and Brit did what any thoughtful daughter-in-law would do—prepare a triple scotch for him. I reached Jay when I finally left my office, and he didn't sound so good. He couldn't remember if I knew about his being a sperm donor in grad school and was really worried about how I would take the news. I reminded him of our dinner out years earlier that he'd paid for with his donor dough.

In the brief time between my getting off the phone with Laura, finishing up in my office, and getting on the road to call Jay, Brit had logged into Jay's 23andMe account. Before getting my call, Brit informed him that he also had a biological daughter in Toronto, Canada. Now Jay and I were talking about his *two* new children: Will and Sabrina. I was laughing. Jay really didn't seem to know if he thought this was good news or bad, and wasn't sure how I might feel about it yet.

"Why are you laughing?" he moaned.

"Honey, I have always wanted a big family. Look what you are giving me! It isn't even my birthday," I chirped.

He asked if I thought it would be okay to reach out and call these kids. I think he was asking me not only if I thought it was a good idea, but also if it bothered me. I thought it was unbelievably cool, and I was super curious. I had a feeling these kids not only wouldn't mind if Jay reached out, but were also probably hoping and waiting for his call.

VIII

MEET THE KIDS

"Today you are you! That is truer than true!
There is no one alive who is you-er than you!"
—Dr. Seuss (aka Theodore Seuss Geisel) (1904-1991)
American Children's Author, Illustrator, Political
Cartoonist, Poet, Animator, Screenwriter, Filmmaker

35
THE FIRST BUNCH

WILL—FIRST CONTACT

By the time I got home after talking to Laura on that first day, Jay had already spoken to his first bio-son and pulled up several pictures. It was eerie how similar they looked to each other. Will was thirty, one year older than Sydney, born on the same day as Ari, shared the name of Jay's favorite uncle, and was an architect. He had Jay's chin dimple, the impish glint in Jay's eyes, the same wiry but sturdy build, and the same broad, unrestrained, welcoming smile. He was married, lived in Peculiar, Missouri, and had two little girls, who were five and three at the time. Jay and Will spoke for a while, comparing ailments and allergies, similarities and differences.

They completely connected right off the bat, but Will also was sensitive to not wanting to intrude on our family and was especially worried about how I felt about all this. If he knew who I was, he would have had no reason to worry at all. He originally started his search wanting to know Jay's health history and had decided for himself, before they spoke, that that would be enough, and for that he would be grateful. Jay was happy to tell Will that he had all his teeth, a full head of hair, and took no medications, all with a bit of playful mischief in his tone. They laughed a little together, and the ice was broken. Jay also told Will that I had encouraged him to reach out and that we and our children were open to exploring any relationship that he or any other bio-kids were interested in.

They ended the conversation with a follow-up scheduled for the following week. Jay passed Will's contact information to me, Sydney, and Brit, and we all sent brief welcome notes by text, fully loaded with playful emojis. We kept Ari and Eric in the loop, but both of them were away at school at the time. Ari was studying acting in New York, and Eric was in graduate school studying law, but all of us were fascinated and excited to learn more about these new "family members."

SABRINA—THE PLOT THICKENS, AND MORE GOOD NEWS

After speaking with Will, Jay reached out to Sabrina. Sabrina was also thrilled to hear from Jay and understandably nervous. She, too, had been searching for her biological father through 23andMe as well as through Ancestry.com, and was not counting on actually having a relationship with him, but really wanted to know where her DNA was from.

When Sabrina was sixteen, she was deeply worried about her father's health. He was quite ill and had begun kidney dialysis. She desperately wanted to help him and thought she might be able to donate her kidney, blood, or some other part of her that might prolong his life. Without her parents' knowledge Sabrina went to her family doctor, who also was treating her dad, to be tested. The lab results came back that Sabrina did not share the same blood type as her father—not only that, but they did not share the same DNA.

Sabrina described feeling shocked and confused, but she wasn't angry. "My relationship with my father was like no other; we were very close. He was my everything."

Because her father was so ill and because of her tremendous love, she kept this secret to herself for years. As if this wasn't painful enough, Sabrina's mom was dealing with her own complex health issues, including lung disease.

Six years later, when Sabrina was twenty-one, she was making coffee in the kitchen with her dad, and her mother was within earshot. "Just as casual as talking about the weather, my dad blurts out that he was not able to conceive," she said.

He went on to explain that her mother and he had agreed their only hope to have a baby was to use a sperm donor. At that time and in their community, fertility wasn't something that people talked about, and theirs was a very private and intimate decision. They agreed to tell no one, including Sabrina.

It took three attempts before Sabrina's mother became pregnant. The procedure was very costly, and her parents knew that this third attempt would be their last, one way or the other. They were down to their last nickels and pennies, but the third time was the charm. All they "knew" about Jay was that he was a tall, white musician *(what?)* with dark hair from New York.

Overhearing the conversation between her husband and daughter, Sabrina's mom cycloned into the kitchen, asking what was going on. Sabrina's dad apparently had very "vivid, piercing blue eyes" and used them to his advantage. He looked bashfully at Sabrina's mom and said, "Oops."

At that point, all the long-hidden conversations spilled out. Truth and more truth came forward. Sabrina divulged that she had known for years, but understood none of it. She was thoroughly fascinated, never angry. She became curious about what the other half of her DNA was made of. She wondered who her biological father might be.

"What does he look like? Why did he become a sperm donor?"

She wondered if she might no longer be an only child.

Sabrina's mother was understandably concerned. She worried that maybe this information would diminish Sabrina's love for the father who raised her, her real father. To the contrary, Sabrina felt that with her father's openness, her love for him only deepened.

"I was his everything. He made sure I knew this, always."

Sabrina shared her news only with her closest friends and the man who would later become her husband, Mike. Nothing was investigated further until years later. On her birthday, a close friend gave her two genetic testing kits. On the outside of the box, she wrote, "Who is your daddy, and what does he do?" Her friend was sensitive to the fact that Sabrina was curious, but also nervous and unsure. She didn't believe she would ever get to know her 'bio-dad,' but wanted to know where she came from and what her background was made of.

"Of course, it would have been amazing to know who the donor dad was and what he looked like, but we never thought in a million years I would find him so easily."

Sabrina was now separated from her first husband and had a little girl named Vienna, in tribute to her much-loved maternal grandmother who came from Austria. Raised in a Catholic home, imagine her surprise when Sabrina learned that she was 49 percent Eastern European Jewish.

Sabrina's response: "Holy. Crap. I found him, and he's Jewish."

Her grandparents had lived in Austria during World War II. They were devastated by the war. Her grandfather harbored Jewish soldiers of the resistance, despite terrible risk to him and his family's safety. The Jewish soldiers taught Sabrina's grandfather Yiddish and about Jewish customs and culture. At the end of the war, Sabrina's grandparents immigrated to Canada to build a new home. They passed on to Sabrina their belief that Jewish people, like all, were to be respected and admired. Her grandparents were staunch in this belief.

Sabrina asked her mother if she had known that her sperm donor was Jewish. Her mother's jaw dropped, and she simply stated, "No." Reviewing her DNA test, in print, it clearly stated:

"Jay Grossman—Predicted Relationship:
Father. You and Jay share 49.7% of your DNA."

Sabrina made several attempts to contact Jay through the messaging service provided by 23andMe, but got no reply. She was clear in her messages that she had a father she loved very much, but wanted to know something about Jay, maybe get a photo? And by the way, thanks for the sperm. Months passed and, hearing nothing, she gave up hope that she'd ever hear from Jay.

Then Sabrina received another message on the Ancestry website from her first biological sister, Liz. Liz and she formed an instant connection, texting back and forth for months. They Googled Jay's name, and a "celebrity dentist" popped up. They thought that this clearly couldn't be their bio-dad.

"Our musician dad's probably a street performer, living off the grid."

But then, one night when Sabrina was out drinking with friends, she received a notification. It was an email from Dr. Jay Grossman. When they finally had that fateful first phone conversation, Sabrina was struck by how confident Jay seemed, but I know he was at least as nervous as she was. Regardless of his worry, his warmth and love won out. He told Sabrina, as he would tell each new bio-kid, that he was available in whatever way he could be, and that his life was an open book with the blessings of his family.

When Jay heard Sabrina's story, he was deeply moved. We were all moved by how deep parental love is, and by the reality that ultimately biology has very little to do with love. As a social worker and psychoanalyst, I knew this intellectually, but I felt it palpably hearing Sabrina's story and as I got to know each of Jay's bio-children. As our donor kids were beginning to make clear to us, biology can feel relevant when and if health questions arise, but it does not replace the love of parents who do all the parenting. Paradoxically, it was indeed biology that brought all our bio-kids to us, but the feelings that began to develop with them wasn't because of obligation to *blood*. For me, there is no biological connection, but I do love these new kids and their families. The superpower of love is evident yet again.

In pictures, it was hard to see where there were physical similarities between Jay and Sabrina, but a year later, when we all met in person, we saw Sabrina had a single dimple in her cheek like Sydney, was so tall like Jay's side of the family, and had the thick, curly hair and hazel eyes that were so familiar to all of us. At the same time, so much in her face reflected her beautiful mother.

In that first call with Jay, Sabrina mentioned that she'd spoken already with Will. She also told him that she had discovered and been speaking with a biological sister she'd located through Ancestry. This didn't register for Jay at first. Sabrina went on and told Jay how lovely she seemed. Still, Jay was not really getting the point, but felt happy for Sabrina that she had spoken with her sister. Eventually Sabrina spelled out that her biological sister was another biological child of Jay's.

"You are telling me that I have another child out there? Might she want to speak with me?" Jay asked.

"As a matter of fact, yes, she would."

Sabrina showed her dad photos of her bio-siblings and Jay. His reaction was to grin and chuckle, "That poor bastard woke up one day and found out he has a bunch of kids running around out there." I wish I could have met him. Several months before we met Sabrina, her father passed away. May his memory always and forever be a blessing.

LIZ (ELIZABETH)—AND NOW WE ANTICIPATE ONLY THE BEST

It's funny, but there was so much about Liz that reminded me of Jay— and strangely, myself—right off the bat. Their first call took place on the same day as the calls with Will and Sabrina. Liz seemed so pleased, but we noticed the nervousness we had come to expect when the kids met not only their bio-dad, but the whole family that comes with him. Jay was ready to share his health history again. He was also getting good at condensing his story, including our life together and what led him to donate his sperm in the first place, into a couple paragraphs.

Liz, too, had started her search with a desire to discover more about her health history, but also wondered if there might be the potential for any meaningful relationship with her bio-dad. She had recently lost her mother in a battle against breast cancer, and her father had left the family several years earlier. Despite hardship, Liz seemed to live her life optimistically, with joy and a great sense of humor. She told Jay that her parents had difficulty conceiving, but she wasn't told until she was much older that her father wasn't biologically her father.

When Liz's mother was originally diagnosed with cancer, Liz was only seven years old. Her mom was diagnosed with inflammatory breast cancer and wasn't expected to survive long. There is less than a 2 percent survival rate past five years with this diagnosis. It was a miracle that she survived for many more years.

During those early childhood years, Liz explained that her father was very supportive, juggling commutes to Manhattan every day from Long Island and being the sole income provider of the family. He was present at the hospital every day while Liz's mom underwent treatment, and also had to be home to raise Liz and her little sister.

Liz and her family got through that original diagnosis of cancer. Eighteen years later, when Liz left home for college, she learned her parents were divorcing. Sometime after this, her father remarried a woman who was unsupportive and jealous of his connections with his daughters and Liz's mother. This led to a complete disintegration over time of their relationship, ending in estrangement.

When Liz was twenty-five, she received the dreaded news that her mom's cancer had returned, and the recurrence was in her pancreas. Her oncologist recommended that Liz get tested genetically for the BRCA mutation. She did and discovered she was indeed BRCA positive. She shared this with her mother's cousin, who kept insisting that Liz really had to speak to her parents about her genetic history—all was not as it seemed—and that it wasn't just about BRCA. But this cousin could say no more without betraying Liz's mother and could only redirect her back to her parents.

Liz got the hint and started to have further questions about her genetic inheritance. She reached out to her father again after a period of very strained, barely-existent contact to find out if he might be willing to do a paternity test so her genetic information could be complete going forward. He was willing and did the test. He seemed to be as shocked as Liz was by the results. Liz was not his biological child.

Liz's parents had been encouraged to keep trying to conceive, even while they were receiving donation injections, and never knew for sure whether they had conceived on their own or not. Once they learned they were pregnant, Liz's parents asked the doctor whether it had been because of their own efforts or because of the intrauterine insemination. The doctor's response was, "What does it matter? You're pregnant, and you're going to be parents!"

This was not an uncommon medical response a few years back, but we know now that the truth is so important. With her new truth, Liz's curiosity was kindled. Because her mother had already passed away by the time she began looking for her biological father, and the father who had raised her had cut contact with Liz with his new marriage, Liz was nervous but eager to find Jay.

Before Liz and Jay ever spoke, Liz found and connected first with Sabrina. Together, they would chat and wonder about who their bio-dad might be. Next to join their conversation was Will. They pooled their information, and Liz found Jay at some point on Facebook and on his website. Jay has some video footage of himself on his website, and Liz was drawn to his mannerisms and way of talking. His expressiveness and posturing were oddly similar to some of her own mannerisms.

Sabrina reached out to Liz and told her, "Shit, I found our dad, and he's cool."

Liz was nervous but also relieved to hear her bio-dad seemed to be an okay guy, and that he had been great with Sabrina on the phone.

At some point during the first conversation Liz and Jay had, I got on the phone to reassure her she was not interloping or interfering. To the contrary, Jay, our kids, and I were all interested and excited to get to know her and her bio-siblings. She wound up describing to me how she'd watched videos of Jay and noticed similarities—she thought they had the same mouth. I've come to know that this was true in more ways than just physical. They are both witty, charming, and know how to throw around sarcasm.

Liz was living in New York City and grew up in Long Island, not far from where Jay grew up. She certainly had some of those Jay Grossman physical attributes, again with a chiseled chin that hinted at a cleft, a similar facial structure, and hazel eyes. Like our son Ari, she was an actress, and juxtaposed to Ari's being the youngest in the family, Liz was the oldest. They now kid around about being the artistic "bookends." The rest of us joke around, "So far!"

We learned that Liz worked also as a nanny, was deeply in love with a wonderful college professor of literature, and lived in SoHo. She candidly voiced her interest in meeting us if we were ever in New York.

"Had we mentioned that your youngest brother is going to school right now in New York for acting?" Jay asked.

There was a lot of warmth, laughter, and familiarity from the beginning, as there was with each new child.

Unfortunately, Liz and I shared a similarity we would rather not have. We talked quite a bit about being BRCA positive and its impact on our lives. I also shared with her how I'd been an actress in college and how I was eager to learn more about what she was doing and where she was headed in life.

PUTTING IT ALL TOGETHER

Before discovering more kids, we had an opportunity to start meeting this first group. Our first face-to-face contact came with Jay's birthday in July of that year, 2018. We thought it would be great to have all these new "children" at the party I was planning for Jay, but Liz and Sabrina couldn't make it. I thought that, in addition to their scheduling constraints, maybe they wanted Will to test the water first. Will and his wife, Monica, accepted the invitation. They would come out and spend a long weekend with us.

Our first sight of each other was amazing. It was weirdly like looking at someone we'd always known, but had never met before. We started with all sorts of stories about how Jay and Will each had grown up. They compared favorite things and pet peeves. Their body language was eerily similar. Will, it seemed, had gotten a big dose of Jay's genetic code.

Sydney and Brit had moved in with us to save up for a house after the baby came, so they were also there when Will and Monica arrived. They had been conversing by text for weeks leading up to the visit and had a warm connection before they even arrived. When our boys came over and met Will and Monica for the first time, it was also easy, funny, and wonderful. Eric's law school was just over an hour away, so he came home for the party, and Ari was home for the summer from college. Everyone was compelled to just stare at each other. We were all so mesmerized. There would be some chatter and then some staring, more chatter then more staring. And, of course, there were some texts and phone calls extended to Liz and Sabrina, keeping them up to date on all that was unfolding.

The big birthday party came where I had invited seventy-ish of our closest family and friends. It was a fully catered event with lots of people who were eager to meet this bio-son, and perhaps a few who were skeptical about how we were extending ourselves. A few people worried in the beginning that we could get hurt by letting Jay's bio-children in, or were concerned that Jay's "traditional" family—me, Syd, Eric, and Ari—could feel threatened or jealous by these newcomers. Nothing could be further from the truth, and Will and Monica confirmed my hope that our meeting would be meaningful and only a beginning. They were a pleasure and really good sports. They graciously met everyone who wanted to speak with them. There was a lot of warmth and love flowing that day.

When people asked me how it was that I could be so open and happy about "Jay's donor children," my response was automatic. If it hadn't been for guys like Jay paving the way for families dealing with infertility issues or non-traditional families, Sydney and Brit wouldn't have been able to conceive their baby. Thank goodness for sperm and egg donors. Secondly, this was actually my dream come true. If the bio-kids would allow, I would welcome them with open arms as part of the large family I had always wanted. Likewise, I never wanted to step on the toes of the families who were really their families. But I'm always of the school that more is better where love is concerned, and believe strongly in inclusivity.

At one point, I sat watching, listening, taking it all in, seeing Sydney's belly starting to grow, all "our kids" together, thinking, *This is really good, and I think it's just going to get better and better.*

I suppose that is the mindset I have worked to develop over the course of my life.

We were so sad when it was time for Will and Monica to leave. We had seen a few photos and videos of them with their two children, who were three and five years old at the time, and were aching to meet them. We hoped they could come back soon and bring Brielle and Keely. We were assured that the girls would love meeting us all, and maybe they would like our chickens most of all. We happen to have a dozen chickens whom we love, and there's rarely a child who meets our chickens and isn't instantly smitten. Soon after they got back home, the texts started flying. Our next date was set for early November to meet the girls. It really could not have gone better.

36
THE SECOND BUNCH

JORDAN—PRACTICALLY OUR NEIGHBOR

A few weeks after Jay's birthday, Brit came running out of the home office, excited and smiling.

"We have another bio-sibling," she announced. "Jordan."

I should mention that somewhere along the line, when Sydney was pregnant, Jay had been talking about needing an executive personal assistant and wasn't having much luck finding one. Brit said that she had given it a lot of thought and felt that this could be a really exciting, mutually beneficial position for her. She made a great case for herself, and after Jay and I discussed it privately, we agreed. She would become his E.P.A. With this, she also took on the responsibility of checking Jay's 23AndMe regularly. She was as excited about this ever-growing family as any of us, and loved managing all the technical components, and Jay and I have been happy to encourage her.

We were all excited about Brit's latest discovery and couldn't resist looking Jordan up on Facebook. Then we couldn't help but compare her with Jay, Will, Liz, and Sabrina, along with my first three babies. I thought that Jordan shared a lot of similarities with Sabrina—her face shape and the "vibe" of her broad smile. Of course, there were also the hazel eyes and dimpled cleft chin.

Jordan lived in Arizona, but often visited California. She and her husband, James, had a girlfriend, Sarah, who lived in Ojai, California, at the time. All three were warm and open about their non-traditional, three-person relationship. Jordan found out that she wasn't genetically related to her father after Sarah gave her a genetic online test to take. It was just for fun, a lark. A few weeks later, she found out that she was Jewish, and that there was a high probability that Dr. Jay Grossman was her father.

Reading her results, she was puzzled and called her mother to ask why her 23andMe says she is Jewish. Her mother said she would be right over. Jordan's mom explained that she had wanted children and had had a difficult time getting pregnant. She and her dad decided to try to conceive using a sperm donor. When she got pregnant, she and her dad didn't see the need to explain this to the children. Jordan had always been wanted and loved, and she was theirs.

Jay reached out to Jordan, and it turned out she would be in Los Angeles and could come spend a Saturday afternoon hanging out and getting to know all of us.

Jordan and James came over for brunch, although Sarah wasn't able to make it to this initial meet-up. Little did we know, Jordan and James had seen on Facebook that Jay loves Duckhorn Cabernet Sauvignon, and was that a hit when they showed up, bottle in hand wrapped with a bow. Jordan told us about her family and how she had been born in Missouri, near Will, before moving to Arizona as a girl. She, like her new brother Will, was an architect who specialized in interior architecture. In addition to being agile with her hands like her bio-dad, she had a deep love for animals and, like me, had chickens at her home. Again, the connections we made that day were fast and potent, and we fantasized about a day where all the bio-sibs, Grossmans, and Sharons—Sydney and Brit—could gather together in one spot, share stories, and celebrate the gift of life and family.

HILARY—ANOTHER NEW YORKER

Hilary and Jay found each other not long after having met Jordan. Hilary was another New Yorker, recently married. She was overjoyed to find out she was not biologically related to the father who had raised her. He had been a destructive force in her family's life, and once he left, she had felt relieved. She was free then to fully enjoy the love and nurturing of a wonderful mother and extended family. We didn't know it at the time, but her enthusiastic, unconditionally supportive grandmother was to quickly become the quintessential grandma of the whole bio-gang.

Hilary discovered her biological connection to Jay much like Jordan, by taking the 23andMe test for fun. When she found out who her bio-dad was and started to connect with all of her bio siblings, she was relieved and thrilled. She was so happy to find out that Jay wasn't a criminal or bad guy like the father she had known as a girl, and that he and his family were welcoming and completely excited by this whole situation. She quickly realized a lot of similarities with her newfound bio-family. She and Jordan wound up spending time together, and James, Jordan's husband, videoed them walking together from behind. Her walk was Jay's walk, flat feet pointed out, a little sway and bounce with each step. Hilary's face was the same shape as Sabrina's and Jordan's. When we finally met Sabrina, we all decided Hilary is a mini Sabrina: Sabrina stood 5'10" and Hilary, 5'3".

Soon all the bio-siblings would be comparing notes about flat feet, how they liked the temperature of a room when they slept, and who was interested in what as kids. They all came to see the striking persistence of the Grossman dimple: two had cheek dimples and the rest all in the chin. All the kids have hazel eyes like Jay. Only Eric, out of all his children, has different eyes—my brown eyes. Although Hilary achieved success in real estate, she felt an affinity with Jay when she discovered his deep commitment to the homeless through his philanthropy. When she learned about Homeless Not Toothless, she envisioned herself contributing and supporting it somehow. She was eager to meet Jay and his family the next time we were in New York, and that would come to pass quite quickly.

MAX—THE LAST SO FAR

The last bio-child to reach out was Max. He had been curious about his biological beginnings, having been raised by his two moms. With Max, it felt like a completion of some cosmic circle. Jay had given to Max's mothers, as a donor had so recently given to Sydney and Brit. We were very moved when we got to really talk to and spend time with Max.

Jay and I had been at a wedding early in the spring, and although I had my phone with me, I had turned it off and put it away for the ceremony. On that particular night, when I pulled out my phone, there were thirty-six messages. For a minute I was worried, then I read quietly for the next five minutes, my heart picking up speed as I went on.

Sydney had watched the documentary, *Three Identical Strangers*, about triplets who were given up for adoption at birth, separated, and given to three different families only to find each other when they were college age. Sydney was inspired from the movie to check on her dad's 23andMe account "for shits and giggles," and—bam! New kid!

I'm not sure who had the last giggle, but the conversation that followed had me in tears from laughter. Sabrina wanted to "know everything," while Hilary logged into her 23andMe account to see that Max had also shown up on her profile: "Half-brother, father's side, 23.4% DNA shared." She immediately declared that she already loved him. Will chimed in and wanted to know how close he might live to Hilary, as they both lived in Long Island. Pictures of Max with his fiancée were added to the communication. Vows were declared to try not to overwhelm him and swamp him with contact, but that barely lasted the first night. Sydney hated that everyone lived so far apart from one another and wanted everyone to come over for dinner and to strategize about introducing Max to everyone.

Sabrina took the first step to reach out personally and privately in that first hour of rapid-fire texting and excitement, giving Max a brief introduction and telling him that "he couldn't have landed in a better family." Someone else shot out a message to the big family group, "He better be cool," evoking a few "haha's" from the group. Hilary wished he would answer already—it had already been two minutes. It started to occur to them that they might want to make a welcome letter template as more siblings might pop up.

All of these texts were what I found when I checked my phone at the reception of the wedding we were attending.

There was a comment from Brit, who was clearly doing some of her signature investigative work on Facebook, discovering Max was a special education teacher. She posted her update with three streaming-tears emojis and one heart emoji. Monica found the perfect GIF: a man with a totally spinning head, and her accompanying comment was that she thought that was probably how Jay would feel when he got this string of texts. She wasn't far off.

It was at that point that Jay and I joined the conversation. I told Jay that he might want to look at his phone. We explained to our friends at the table that some unusual news had come up, and we shared the details, apologizing for having our phones out. They were intrigued and wanted us to carry on so they could learn more. We were texting our kids and alternately communicating what was going on with everyone at the table we were seated with. We shared in both conversations how strange it was that our youngest son is Ari Max, and now we have found a Max. Brit, being her hilarious and quick-witted self, picked right up and wondered, "What if Max's middle name is Ari?"

Pretty soon the kids were friending Max on Facebook, guessing about how he might be feeling, and with Jordan being the last to join the conversation, she added the observation that Max had "the chin dimple."

We had a wonderful time at the wedding. Everyone at our table was entertained and laughing with us. The next morning, I was awakened slightly earlier than usual with a text message at 4 a.m.

From Liz: "Waking up to a new brother?! Whaaat." And of course she was excited to hear he wasn't far from her location in Manhattan.

Will, Sabrina, and Liz connected with each other before Jay knew that there were messages waiting for him in his genetic profile. It was months before they heard from Jay. Jordan, Hilary, and Max all had the experience of a shockingly immediate response, not only from their bio-dad, but from what felt like a hoard of bio-sibs and, of course, me. All of them were lovable, warm, engaged, and engaging.

When Jay did reach Max the next day, the connection felt familiar to Jay. Max was tentative but curious and, like the others, warmed up quickly. All the vital information was shared, and then the more spontaneous conversation took shape. Jay shared with Max that we were coming to New York in several weeks for the New York University Dental School graduation at Madison Square Gardens, where Jay was going to be addressing the class and receiving a humanitarian award for his work with the homeless. He asked Max if he might be around to meet. Max said he would be.

The New York gathering consisted of Jay, me, Sydney, Brit, Ari, Hilary, and her husband Andrew, Liz, Max, and Max's fiancée, Laura. Eric unfortunately was winding down his academic year and couldn't afford to get away, so he had to enjoy it all vicariously from Los Angeles. And although Max and Laura couldn't make it in for the graduation during their workweek, we had a great hang-out in our hotel suite, talking for hours, followed by a wonderful dinner at a local neighborhood pub. We talked about our families, old and new. We talked about education, politics, psychology, movies, and art. Max had a lot of facial similarities to Ari, his humor was so like Jay's, and his birthday was the day before mine. There was something ineffable, beyond the commonalities, that seemed to be pulling us all together. The more we spoke, the more we recognized so many shared values, styles, and interests. It was so easy to connect.

Within a week of getting home from our New York trip, Max reached out to us to thank us for dinner and time together. He had been so pleasantly surprised by the loving and authentic reception he'd received from us Grossmans as well as from his bio-sibs, as we've all come to identify the gang. Having met us, he and Laura couldn't see not including us in their wedding and wanted us all to consider coming. We couldn't have felt more honored and privileged.

IX

FROM GENERATION
TO GENERATION

"There are two ways to live: you can live as if nothing is a miracle; you can live as if everything is a miracle."
—ALBERT EINSTEIN (1879-1955)
NOBEL PRIZE-WINNING PHYSICIST

37
CONNECTING

Introductions of all sorts took place over the next year. Jay and I were in New York several times. Whether we were visiting Ari or there for a more formal event like the NYU Dental School Graduation, there were many opportunities to get together with our bio-kids.

Meeting Liz for the first time in New York was exceptionally memorable because we were also celebrating Ari's twenty-first birthday. As I mentioned earlier, Ari was attending college there, so we all met for the occasion at a lovely famed favorite Manhattan restaurant, Daniel. What courage and strength of character Liz had to come and meet not only me and Jay, Syd, Brit, and Ari, but also my parents and sister, Amy. She glided in, blonde hair flowing in our sea of brunette. She was elegant, smiling, and glowing. She confided in us that she had been painfully nervous about meeting us, but she had been in text contact with Will and Monica, who assured her in detail with stories of their stays with us that we were "okay." I wouldn't have guessed by her openness and grace that she was anything but calm and self-assured.

Liz produced 'mommy-to-be' and baby gifts for Sydney and Brit, as well as a birthday gift of the coolest sneakers for Ari. Questions, answers, good food and drink were in abundance. We took a ton of photos, and there were even tears shed. We all wished that Liz's mother was still alive and could have been with us to celebrate.

In the fall, Will and Monica came to visit us again, this time with their beautiful girls in tow. When I got home from work on the day they arrived, they had already settled in, made comfy by Sydney and Brit. I walked into the living room where Keely and Brielle were playing with new toys on the floor. Brielle ran right up to me and gave me the biggest hug as if she'd known me all her life. When Keely saw Brielle's comfort with me, she, too, opened her arms for a big bear hug. She didn't even want to let go. What a weekend we had, collecting chicken eggs and going to a special Haunted Halloween encounter, perfect for young children and old, at a ranch near our home. By the end of the trip, Brielle had dubbed us Papa J and Grandma B, names we hadn't asked for but endeared us to those little girls forever.

After our first meeting with Jordan and James, we discovered they, like us, enjoyed skiing. Although we didn't get to ski together, we did meet up at Mammoth Mountain in the Sierras one weekend and got to go out for a fabulous Greek meal at Jimmy's Taverna, where Chip, our good friend and sommelier, was thrilled to meet our new children and bring us fabulous wines he recommended. It was also the first time Jordan said with a smile, that Jay "parented" her when she came out to our car not wearing a jacket. She assured him that despite the snow falling all around us, she'd be fine going from the car to the restaurant and back. She laughs today and says, "I wasn't actually fine, but the truth is I didn't have a cute enough dinner jacket!"

Jordan and James proved to be as playful and open as we'd found them in our first meeting. We discussed topics that ranged from serious and deep to comical and superficial, from personal and familial to politics and music. We wound up going back to the house where they were staying with friends, and got to meet Sarah, their third partner who hadn't been able to join us for dinner. We proceeded to the snow-blanketed backyard to crawl into their cozy, low-lying, Jordan-designed igloo, where candles were lit, drinks poured, and toasts made.

"To the love of chickens and family."

Clink. Drink.

We started to discuss the possibility that all the bio-kids might want to join our family for our annual 4th of July sojourn in Zion National Park by way of Las Vegas. They were all in.

Next, we met Hilary and Andrew in New York. We met at a little french restaurant downtown and talked the night away. It was amazing to watch Hilary and Jay take each other in. It was very intimate and quiet. It was an instance where time sort of just hung there between us, then passed, but an important connection had formed. Hilary told us of how she had checked up on Jay before meeting us, and was so inspired by Homeless Not Toothless. Participating in a charity like HNT was something she said she would love to get involved in. She told us in greater depth about her family and how relieved she was to find out that the dad who had raised her wasn't her dad because he had been so abusive and neglectful of her mother. She was consoled he had left the family and that Jay and his family brought so much possibility to her life. She thought we would also enjoy meeting her family at some point, and by the end of the evening, we had become Facebook friends with her mother and grandmother.

As the year was coming to a close, the bio-kids were all communicating through every available modality. The kids created an instant-message group thread for the whole family and a family group on Facebook. Plans began to spin and take shape as we considered the possibility of a "family" gathering in Las Vegas and Zion National Park, as well as other ways we might all convene in a group and get to know each other more.

38
A NEW GENERATION

Sydney grew up watching me teach childbirth classes. She was enthralled with birth throughout her childhood—including Ari's birth when she was eight years old—and had seen a lot of birth films before he was born. She loved babies and children as she grew up, always the loving older cousin role, babysitting in her teens, and working briefly as a nanny in her early twenties.

She hoped that one day, when she had her own child, I would teach her and her significant other The Bradley Method for childbirth, and that I would be there with her. Now here she was, ready with her wife to start her journey into parenthood. As she went through her pregnancy, she found herself getting closer and closer to her newfound sisters and sister-in-law in particular, but surrounded by the love of her brothers as well. The excitement was loud and wonderful.

Sydney had a general idea of how she hoped the birth of her baby would unfold because she had been around my classes and birth all her life. Brit was a youngest child, though, and had not had a lot of contact or education yet about birth and parenting, but was open. I wound up teaching a small class to Sydney, Brit, and another couple who were among their best friends. At first, Sydney and Brit thought they would either have a hospital or birthing center birth. They thought that our house was probably too remote for a safe home birth, but still they were open to learn and find their way toward what would be best for them and their baby.

By the end of the twelve-week course, Sydney was prepared to undertake the athletic event of birth, and Brit was prepared as her coach. As part of their journey and learning, they found a certified nurse midwife they really loved, and chose to have the baby at home. There would not be any disruptive transfers to the hospital during the most difficult part of labor, only nestling in at home and laboring wherever she wanted, pushing wherever was comfortable, and supported only by those who were closest to her and trained.

An important note about Sydney is that she never does anything late. Friends, family, siblings, and bio-sibs were all a-chatter about when this baby would come: early, late, or on time. Only 4 percent of all babies come on their due date, so I did try to help Sydney and Brit keep perspective that this baby could likely come two weeks before or two weeks after her due date, or any time in between. The important thing was that this baby would come when she was ready. Did I mention they discovered they were having a girl? Gifts from the bio-sibs were cute, sweet, and hilarious. I especially loved Sabrina's gift: a onesie bearing the Canadian maple leaf.

Sydney and Brit had planned so much so beautifully. Everyone who was to attend would have a role. One of my good friends, Anne, who was also a Bradley instructor, came to stay with us in our home a week before the baby's due date, as per Sydney's wishes. Sydney thought it would be helpful if my best friend, Ilana, could be there specifically as *my* support person, making sure I had water and remembered to take breaks to pee, but also as another wise, loving, Bradley mommy. Brit's mother was there to support Brit and be in charge of nourishment for everyone. Jay was the birth-tub filler-upper and all-around support person, also an expert Bradley daddy. Our friend Steve was counted on as lower-back support with his expertise in shiatsu. They also hired a photographer who happened to be a doula. For the main event, Leslie, the midwife, was there with Blyss, her backup, who also happened to be a fully licensed nurse midwife. Sydney and Brit, had created a web of amazing support and strength for the birth of their baby.

On Saturday December 1st, Sydney's due date, I had an eye doctor appointment, and Brit, Anne, and Jay were participating at Jay's office in a Homeless Not Toothless day. I had just paid my bill and was walking out of my doctor's office when I felt my phone vibrate. "Missed Call," from Sydney. I called her right back, expecting her to ask me to pick up milk or bananas at the market.

She answered after the first ring and calmly told me that maybe perhaps it was possible she might be in labor.

"What are your symptoms?" I asked easily as I walked to my car.

She wasn't hurting, but felt some pulling in her lower abdomen. I had taught her that pregnant women start having contractions very early in pregnancy but often don't feel them until their second or third trimester. Toward the end of pregnancy, one way to tell if the contractions were truly labor is to walk a while, and if the contractions don't go away, eat something nourishing. And if they don't go away after that, drink some water. And if they still continue, try taking a shower followed by a nap. If the contractions continue, repeat. One was to go through this sequence until the contractions either went away or picked up in intensity—in which case, it is definitely labor. Sydney had gone through this cycle several times and noticed the contractions weren't subsiding.

"Maybe you want to pick up Brit and Anne and head home, Mom. I think this actually might be labor," she said.

I called Brit, who had spoken earlier to Sydney, and I told her that I'd come and get her and Anne, and we'd go home and see what was what. I was still not convinced she was in labor, but excited to be getting so close.

By the time we got home, Sydney was walking up the street with Brit's mom, who had come over to help Sydney. They both looked pretty happy. Brit hopped out of the car and joined her mom and her wife to walk back to the house. If Sydney was in labor, she was early in the process because she was very chatty and giggly. Later in the game, mothers often pull inward and become very focused on the work at hand.

Sydney was eager to fill me in on how her day had been going so far. The best part was that the contractions weren't going away and seemed to be coming more regularly and steadily. We had lowered the heat in our saline Jacuzzi to body temperature, and Sydney thought it "might be nice to labor there for a while."

"Okay," I told her as Brit and I walked away from her and she started toward the Jacuzzi, "we'll go get our bathing suits and come out and join you in a minute."

That was not to be. Brit was a bit in front of me and was already out of earshot, but I heard an insistence in Sydney's voice as she said, "Mom, another contraction is coming. Get in the pool now!"

I have found that it isn't helpful or wise to argue with a laboring woman, so in an instant I threw off my clothes and was naked in the pool with my naked Sydney, coaching her through the first of the many contractions that would bring her daughter.

Brit returned a contraction or two later in her bathing suit, offering up my bathing suit as well. Modesty might have been irrelevant to Syd at that point, but I was happy to have the cover of my bathing suit regardless. Sydney slipped into a rhythm of relaxation quickly. Between Brit, me, and Anne, we were massaging her, giving her verbal coaching, and timing contractions. We quickly became an organic group of women working together in what felt like the most ancient and primal of ways to support Sydney and the baby. We probably would have stayed in the water much longer, except that during one mighty contraction the water in the Jacuzzi became murky with what seemed to be a pop within Sydney's body. Her water had broken. We decided to get out of the tub, walk a little, eat and drink a little, and maybe lay down together a little in my bed—a little. All of these changes in activity brought on the strength and closeness of her contractions. Her body was doing what it needed to do.

I asked Sydney if she might want to labor on the yoga ball and pick things up a bit. She was beginning to go more within herself, wanting quiet and to close her eyes. She quietly agreed that the yoga ball might be helpful. She had begun to feel hot and cold alternately, and couldn't figure out at times which one she was. I wrapped her up in a soft blanket, my arms around her, rocking, bouncing, and singing to her as she labored. The effect of the gentle bouncing was powerful. I reminded her that when she and baby surrendered at the same time to the process of birth, that's when the baby comes.

I encouraged Sydney to speak aloud or silently to baby and let her know that everything was okay and not to be afraid, to encourage and reassure her. We reconvened in my bed. Sydney was singing a low, deep guttural labor song that I joined her in, and soon so did Brit, Anne, and Ilana. Steve, who had also shown up with his magical hands, and offered a lot of relief to Sydney, who was having labor pain in her lower back, also sang.

By early evening, her contractions were two to three minutes apart, and I suggested that Brit contact the midwife and photographer. Given that this was Sydney's first labor, the midwife figured she had some time to get to our house before Sydney would be ready to actually push the baby out. She was going to stop at her office to pick up some paperwork, then come over. I told Brit that she might want to let the midwife know that I thought Sydney was so relaxed her labor and birth would probably move very quickly and she should come directly to us. It was too late, though. She had already gone to her office.

By the time Leslie arrived, Sydney was ready to push. Sydney was relieved because she knew that the strategy in this athletic event had shifted from playing the relaxing game to being able to get in there and push. She wanted to go downstairs to the birthing pool and see if she felt more comfortable there. The pool had been filled a little too high. That turned out to be somewhat amusing for those around her and annoying for her. When she wanted to push, she instinctively wanted her chin down on her chest, but each time she did this she got water up her nose and in her face. We decided to take note for next time, but for now we had to get her out and move over to our couch.

As Sydney and Brit settled into the rhythms of pushing, Jay got a phone call. It was Cantor Marcelo, the cantor of our Synagogue and a friend of ours.

Jay told him that Sydney was in labor and, "Do you want to come by? It's pretty amazing."

Cantor Marcelo hesitatingly said that he had never been at a birth and wanted to be sure it was okay. Shortly after that, he arrived, guitar in hand, unbeknownst to me. After the cantor had arrived at the house and had been waiting in our living room, apart from the action taking place in the family room, Jay came to me between the contractions that I was intently coaching Sydney through. He let me know that Marcelo was in the living room.

"The living room?" I asked incredulously. "How long has he been there?"

"Mmmm, fifteen, maybe twenty minutes," Jay answered.

I felt so badly that Marcelo hadn't been ushered in to join us. Jay explained that he thought Marcelo wasn't really sure if it was okay to come in. Well, I wasn't having him in the living room, and having checked in with Sydney and Brit, I knew they felt as strongly.

After some helloing and basic pleasantries, I told him he wasn't to sit alone while new life was about to burst in, born from Sydney, a few feet away. I really didn't give him an option, so in he came. The lights were low, the mood was one of love and anticipation. It was quiet, except for Sydney's pushing-song of grunts and effort.

My youngest sister, another Bradley mother, had spoken with Sydney earlier during labor to find out if she and her fourteen-year-old son could come and offer support, and they, too, had joined the community of encouragers. Ilana was holding one of Sydney's feet, and Brit had her other foot. Brit's mom was close by Brit, and Blyss and I were at Sydney's face, coaching, holding, instructing, and loving her. Jay was videoing. Anne was offering support to whoever needed it, wherever it was needed.

Then, the cantor began to play his guitar. He began playing traditional Jewish folk songs and prayers that were part of our Malibu Jewish Center and Synagogue's non-traditional liturgy and playbook. We began singing along. At one point, I couldn't sing or coach because I was crying, tears sliding down my cheeks. Sydney's next contraction began, and she needed me. It was the one time in her labor that she got snappy with me.

"Cut it out, do NOT sing, do not cry, you need to coach me, NOW!" And so I did.

Within an hour of pushing, a small head began to emerge, crowning. Sydney strained against the feeling of doubt and the primordial fear of being torn open, but we reassured her that this was safe, the way it goes. She needed to lean in, push, and surrender. She did. Out came a head, and with Leslie's firm encouragement, Sydney pushed out the baby's shoulders. With Leslie's encouragement, Sydney reached down and brought the baby up to meet her for the first time.

"I fucking did it," was her memorable declaration as she and Brit and everyone else in the room wept with the joy of being present in one of the most sacred moments of life.

The cantor began to sing the prayer that celebrates the miracles of life, particularly the arrival of any long-awaited occasion, the same song we sang at Ari's birth: the Shekhekhianu.

"Thank you, universe, for giving us life, sustaining us, and permitting us to reach this time of divine joy."

Everyone sang and hugged and watched and kissed and oohed and aahed and hugged and kissed some more. Can anyone doubt the extraordinary power of love?

Thea Madison Quin Sharon was born after six hours of labor into the arms of her loving mothers and community—7 pounds, 9 ounces, 25 inches long. She was beautiful, wrapped in the stunning garb of pure newness. She didn't cry. There wasn't anything to cry about. Her eyes were open, and she seemed to take it all in. Within the hour, she had her first meal at her mother's breast, while Sydney took in a hearty meal, celebrating with her first sushi in ten months.

Seeing the heads of the two mommies locked together, forehead to forehead, while they both snuggled and held Thea was one of those simple unforgettable moments that make life matter. Their journey was beginning together. Amazing that this is how we all begin, every one of us. I find it mind-boggling and deeply emotional.

X
THE END

"Breathe. Let go. And remind yourself that this very moment is the only one you know you have for sure."
—Oprah Winfrey (1954-)
American Media Executive, Talk Show Host,
Philanthropist, Actress, Television Producer

39
THE END—
BUT ONLY OF THE BOOK

So much happens in a lifetime.

I continue to have the most magical moments, and hit those bumps we must all hit along the way. My takeaway is that life and all its moments are best met head-on. I haven't shared about all the potholes I've hit—my Graves' disease, snapped tendons, falls, breaks, and breakdowns with my children as they grew up and faced their own bumps. I also haven't included all the magic and miracles that continue to develop as I enter new wonderful places in my personal and professional life: travel, dining, weddings of the bio-kids, or the family trip that we did have to Vegas and Zion that happened to be off-the-hook fabulous. It's not necessary to share everything, but certainly the important thing is to recognize that our lives have rhythm, complete with highs and lows. We love, laugh, and be.

Every day when I wake up, I set my intention for the day, review my goals, meditate, exercise, and take some time to journal. It's the way I stay connected with myself, always wanting to learn and grow.

William Shakespeare encouraged, "To thine own self be true."

And this, with love and laughter, has driven my life. I focus on my truest desires in life and refuse to settle for mediocrity. No one wants to be on their deathbed at the end of a lifetime and feel that they haven't lived fully; I certainly don't. We don't want to leave anything on the table. I have places to go and people to love.

I see that the happiness, love, and freedom I have in my life is directly correlated to my commitment to know myself, to be known by others, and to know others all on a foundation of love, curiosity, and integrity. When I asked my parents questions as a little girl, they told me the truth. It didn't go so well for me when I ran it by Dougie next door, but I learned how important it is to be sensitive to the emotional and intellectual world of others. How awful it must be to be afraid of words, curiosity, and truth.

I would go slower and be more sensitive in the future, but I have spent my life being curious and open in the pursuit of understanding both actual and personal truth. Actual truth is absolute: one plus one equals two. Personal truth is relative: discovering and embracing what makes us "us" and how we put it all together. Personal truth has the capacity to grow and expand over the course of a lifetime. This idea and feeling helped me navigate the terrifying waters of cancer; I was able to grow and develop a love for myself that included my lost and diseased cells.

When I was diagnosed with cancer, my initial reflex was to want to pull away from myself. I was terrified and angry. I needed the help of family, friends, and my medical team to engage me in the pursuit of expanding myself to include my cancer. I needed love and help to stay conscious about my commitment to life. Simple as it may sound, committing to life and love really are the two elements it takes to have an extraordinary life. Sometimes we need help to stay on that path and remain grounded in integrity.

One day, I was lying on the couch in my first analysis. I remember crying and announcing that I just wish I could grow up and do it all myself already. I was twenty-two at the time. Will I ever be able to just do "it" myself?

My analyst commented on how sad and frustrated he could clearly hear I was, then said, "I think perhaps it is the 'little you' that has a fantasy about what it is to be a grown-up. Children think that being a grown-up is to do it all yourself, as you imagine Mommy and Daddy do. But Mommy and Daddy don't do it all themselves; they rely on each other. Being a grown-up is realizing the pleasure that comes from relying on one another, and knowing that we don't have to do 'it' by ourselves."

This is an idea that has resonated with great significance for me ever since.

Thank goodness I found Jay. He is my helpmate, and I am his, and together we discover over and over how great it is to know that being a grown-up is about being able to help each other, while also feeling great about ourselves separately.

Life is all about the love we make and share. That's not to say we don't have painful, enraging, or frustrating experiences, or differences in opinions and perspectives, but our "salvation" and happiness relies on our ability to connect with ourselves and others in meaningful ways. It's about our capacity to love, laugh, and be.

What is it that keeps us from taking the clear steps that are recommended by the self-help community, parents, or personal and business advisors that guarantee improvement and happiness? I think the answer lies in the realm of what we don't know that we don't know. Said simply, it's the unconscious stuff.

In my upbringing with my psychoanalytic, loving parents, the unconscious was always being attended to, directly or indirectly. My parents would ask me about my dreams and help me understand what I might be thinking about or struggling with that I didn't consciously know I was struggling with. The funny thing was that as soon as they pointed out the unconscious element and put a name to it, I felt immediate relief. The underlying message I got was that I was loved and it was okay and important to incorporate my feelings with my thinking. This has since been fundamental in navigating every twist and turn in my life. I believe that cultivating, receiving, and expressing love is a superpower. This is available to anyone who reaches for it, and that is all I've done to fuel my success and happiness.

I had pain and grief along the way. I needed help at times, as we all do, and I chose to go to people with expertise. I had my parents, teachers, sisters, and friends. I found people at different times who helped me better see what was in my unconscious mind, and also understand the influences of my unconscious on my conscious. I found psychoanalysts, both in my early adulthood and then again as I began training as a psychoanalyst myself, who encouraged me to lead the way in our work and helped me to hear and know myself. And, of course, I found Jay. Together we created a life we love and a love that we only want to grow and deepen with each moment we have together. I think that it's because of my relationships and all that they have encouraged me to be that I have become resilient but strong, courageous but vulnerable, and enjoyed and lived such an amazing life.

As I reflect on the ups and downs and in-betweens, I believe my life has been wonderful—not because of the absence of trouble, but because of the presence of it. Adversity is interwoven with joy and accomplishment. I have learned from everyone, personally and professionally, that adversity helps us to grow if we allow it to. Resisting adversity and pretending we don't have to include it or regard it leads us into weeds of despair, anger, and disappointment. I believe our unconscious world plays an integral role throughout life. Unconsciously, my love for people was always what brought me around to becoming a successful therapist, childbirth educator, author, wife, mother of three, and now mother of nine, traditional grandma to Thea, and not-so-traditional grandma to Brielle, Keely, and Vienna.

There are days I feel I could burst out of my skin with the delight and love I feel. I am not afraid to die, and feel in every moment I am so complete and full—but I do love being alive, and I hope I have a whole lot more time on the planet to love, be loved, and make a difference.

The to-dos offered by the great self-help gurus out there are most accessible when we are most in touch with our unconscious, our palette of emotional experience, and our capacity to think it all out consciously. I suppose at the end of the day I have brought aspects of my unconscious to bare on the content of this memoir, and the result is a roadmap to anybody's success and happiness. This is not about what to do as much as a transparent sharing of what 'being' might look like—and for each of us, being is different. I hope that in the end, this book makes you smile and feel happy about all that is possible for you in love, laughter, and being.

THE END

ACKNOWLEDGMENTS

Jay Grossman, you are my constant reader. You have encouraged me to write every step of the way, and then read every draft. You have listened to me struggle over whether or not I have chosen the right phrase or word. To publish or not to publish, that was the question. But you kept cheering me on. I am clear that you love me unconditionally, and with that, you always bring your honest opinions and input. Thank you.

Mom and Dad, you have always encouraged my every undertaking, and my thanks extends far beyond, but includes, your constant love, support, and honest feedback.

Sydney Sharon, my daughter, thank you for helping me with every technical and artistic challenge. Your creativity and expertise have been indispensable. Your leadership and willingness to be on my production team in any and every way possible has touched me deeply. I am so proud of you.

Ari and Eric my sons, thank you for taking an interest and time to review and provide helpful and important feedback. Ari your final reviews and editorial comments as I prepared to go to publication were so clear, on point, and insightful. My gratitude is immense.

Ilana Springer, you have held me accountable and listened and encouraged me to write this book for more than ten years, especially when I have been tired and self-doubting. Thank you for being my best friend.

Elle Harriman, for reading and critiquing and bringing your marketing eye, thank you. You were among the first to read the rough draft and bring your fabulous aesthetic to my book cover! I am so happy to have met you and begun our meaningful and loving new friendship.

I can't imagine having finished this book without the collaboration, teamwork, and exquisite literary eye of my Editor, Qat Wanders! Qat and her team at Wandering Words Media, have been nothing short of amazing. Christy Leos started it all with her developmental edits. Christina Bagni and Qat Wanders teamed up in their work on the content editing, and then back it went to Qat for copy editing. Finally, the book was in Allison Goddard's able hands and mind for the proofreading. Editing has been like a skillfully played intricate team sport, but better. You all have taught me so much and helped me to bring my book to publication—no small feat. Thank you.

Kit Karzen, thank you for your amazing photography and capturing me on film for the book cover. I never imagined having so much fun for a photo shoot. And Nicole Simons, what would I do without your eye to dress and finesse me. Thanks for your years of service and love, styling and supporting me.

Lise Cartwright, thank you for coaching, mentoring, and teaching me the technical details of becoming a self-published author. You are gentle but firm, and oh-so knowledgeable. I only hope that this is just our beginning.

Lisa Zelenak and Sean Sumner, thank you. Thank you for nudging me forward, providing a background of structure, coaching, and accountability, and sometimes kicking my ass. You really have been a demand for excellence and brought out the best in me, all while also bringing out some love and laughter. What a journey! I look forward to what our futures have to bring.

Chandler Bold, thank you for founding the Self-Publishing School and reaching out. Hal Elrod, you, your Miracle Morning and Miracle

Equation, were the cherries on top. You reminded me that I had a book or two in me that might make a difference in the world and you directed me to Chandler.

You and Chandler reminded me that "now" is the only time we have, and that there never is a perfect time to publish. I am clear that you both believed in me and all of your students and readers. Thank you from the bottom of my heart. I am living my life at a "10 out of 10" thank you very much.

There are so many others who have supported me and worked with me in bringing this book to fruition: my nine children, my extended family, friends, my mastermind groups, and my launch team. I am so grateful.

My final thanks goes to all the authors who have touched, moved, and inspired me over the course of my life. With a special thanks to Stephen King, who is my favorite author, including his book, On Writing, A Memoir of the Craft.

ABOUT THE AUTHOR

Briar Flicker-Grossman, Psy.D., L.C.S.W., F.I.P.A. has been a practicing psychotherapist for thirty-six years. She has her doctorate in psychoanalysis from The Psychoanalytic Center of California and is a life coach as well as a certified Bradley Method childbirth instructor. She is a proponent of intuitive living and depth psychology, and teaches psychotherapists and coaches.

Briar's mission is to empower people to love, laugh, and "be" in their lives through raised consciousness and compassion, one person at a time. She has published articles and blogs on growth, development, pregnancy, parenting, and being. She speaks publicly and openly about her experience of overcoming breast cancer, having a successful thirty-year marriage, love, childbirth, parenting, and intuitive living.

Briar lives in Malibu Canyon, California, with her husband, chickens, and various groupings of children. In her spare time, she hikes, knits, plays guitar, skis, and enjoys time with her family and friends.

CAN YOU HELP?

THANK YOU FOR READING MY BOOK!

I really appreciate all of your feedback,
and I love hearing what you have to say.

Please leave me an honest review on Amazon
letting me know what you thought of the book.

Thanks so much!

Dr. Briar Flicker-Grossman